JOHN OTWAY

Cor Baby, That's Really Me!

KLG Press

This edition published in 2009 by Karen Lawrence Glass
This edition © copyright John Otway
Copyright © 1990 John Otway
First published by Omnibus Press 1990
Re-printed in 1996
Re-printed in 1998 by Cherry Red Books

Printed in Great Britain by CPI Cox & Wyman
Reading, RG1 8EX

Edited by Chris Charlesworth
Art Direction by Lisa Pettibone
Designed by Robert Fairclough
Picture research by Paul Giblin
Typesetting and project co-ordination by Caroline Watson

ISBN 978-0-9564343-0-2

AUTHOR'S NOTE

My spelling are grammar are diabolical. I was aided in the first instance by the spellcheck on my wordprocessor and by Nick Creasy in the second.

Nick spent many months covering my drafts with red ink and sending me home to do my corrections on the promise that there would be rich rewards once this book became a best seller.

John Otway, January 1990.

This book is dedicated to my girls
Karen and Amy

CHAPTER 1

The summer of 1978, John Otway stood on a stage built in the Market Square of his home town Aylesbury. The police had sealed off the town centre, ATV were filming the event for his own 40-minute TV show to be screened on national television, and 10,000 locals turned up to witness the event.

The TV programme was to be called *Stardustman* – about a local dustman who always believed he was a star and went on to make a hit record. The producers of the show hopefully felt that Otway was going to make more than one hit record, and they would have a valuable piece of vintage footage. In the same way, his record company also hoped he would have lots more hits and gave him a quarter of a million pounds in the way of encouragement. Both, along with Otway himself, were to be sadly disappointed.

This is the story of that dustman, who fought tooth and nail to become a star, only to have to fight tooth and nail not to become a dustman again. Parts of it you may find amusing, parts sad, occasionally enlightening but quite often you may just think "What a prat".

There was a very similar feeling among a large group of pupils at The Grange County Secondary School in Aylesbury one winter lunchtime. Our 14-year-old hero had gathered together an audience of 100 to witness him down a complete bottle of ink in one. They stood there speechless as he poured the blue liquid down his throat, and then complained bitterly that he had been given Stevenson's instead of Quink.

A few of the audience found this event amusing, a few sad, the occasional person there who was strangely attracted to this rather odd youth found it enlightening, but quite a lot did think, "What a prat". Their opinion did not change a great deal when Otway complained for days afterwards that his pee had turned blue.

It's true that Otway had a particularly tough childhood, but as one contemporary later explained, "I know it might be wrong to mock the afflicted, but when the afflicted do such bloody stupid things it is difficult not to."

Otway was born at 8.00pm on October 2, 1952 at 17, Whitehall Street, Aylesbury. His sister Margaret, who had just reached the age of two, remarked, "Oh! it's a little Rupert," on first seeing her little infant brother. Apart from this small observation, his introduction to the world was relatively normal.

Within a few years it became pretty obvious this was no normal child. Basically it took Otway twice as long as it would take any normal kid to walk, talk and tie his shoelaces. Other things, like writing legibly or kicking a ball in a straight line, he has not mastered to the present day.

The first five years of his life were as normal as they could be for someone like this. However, when he started school and was surrounded by other kids of his own age, his impediments became more obvious.

It is often noted that young children can be very cruel to children that are different to them in some way. Sending Otway to school was a complete and total proof of this theory. He seemed to have the ability to turn otherwise "nice" kids into sadistic thugs and turn a whole class against him within a couple of days.

"He was pretty horrid," recalls someone who remembers him at the time. "He was awkward, always looked dirty, you couldn't understand a word he said and he did have one of those unfortunate faces you just want to hit."

By the age of eight, his parents were being pressured into sending him off to a school for difficult children, but as his mother explained: "I always felt that John would eventually have to integrate himself, and thought that if he could find a way of coming to terms with his problems in a normal school, he would in the end be better off for it."

Coming to terms in a practical way for John meant going to a speech therapist to learn to talk, having his shoes built up to learn to walk, and learning to punch other kids in the mouth if they gave him too much of a hard time.

Two brothers who were giving John a hard time were Roger (later to be known as Wild Willy) and Jim Barrett, who ran a gang of undesirable thugs in the proximity of the Otway house.

"I don't know why he kept coming round," says Willy now. "Every time he came round he'd get bashed up. No one liked him, and he always ended up going home with a bloody nose or something like that. Eventually, after about a year, he did stop coming around though."

Around this time (between the ages of eight and 10) we see the first stirrings of an interest in music in the young Otway.

Otway's parents and his four sisters moved into a large Victorian house in Wendover Road, and his mother took in other people to make ends meet. There were as many as 14 people living in that house at the same time. It was a constant changing mixture of people: some were moving into new jobs in the area, others were kids who had grown too old to stay in the children's home across the road and needed somewhere to live while they found their feet. One such person – who was dying his hair outrageous colours back in 1961 – was Gordon. He had a profound effect on Otway.

Mrs Otway, unlike John, had a wonderful operatic voice and in her youth had considered becoming a professional singer. She had a love of classical music matched only by her hatred of the new abrasive pop music. To his mother's dismay, and often fury, on Sundays John and Gordon would listen avidly to Alan Freeman's *Pick of the Pops* on what was then called the BBC Light Programme. John was completely fascinated.

Between being bashed up and bashing other kids up at school, Otway discovered, to his amazement, that if he sang the Lonnie Donegan and Cliff Richard songs in the playground, and threw his uncoordinated body around at the same time, pupils bored with the tedium of playtime would stand around and watch. He also discovered that the louder he yelled, and the more he threw his body around, the more kids would gather. After a few playtimes of this, the head teacher Mr Edwards noticed a crowd gathering at one end of the playground and went to investigate.

Not realising that he was the first adult to ever see a John Otway performance he decided, probably quite rightly, that this lad, who was already disruptive enough, was basically being stupid. He immediately stopped the show, took his young pupil aside and gave him some advice. Had he taken it up, it would have changed his whole life.

"John," he said, "What you are doing is showing off, what you are doing looks very silly and everyone in the school is laughing at you."

It was the first, but not the last time, that he was banned from playing. The one thing that Mr Edwards missed that later people picked up on, was that as well showing off and looking silly it also sounded horrible.

Being before the age of the video camera and never having sung in front of a mirror or tape recorder, Otway felt that what he was doing was the same as Cliff and Lonnie. Because people watched him do it, he felt he had the ability and talent to be a star.

"I did worry even at that age that I might not be good looking enough to do what Cliff and Lonnie did though," says Otway now, "But I loved the attention. I remember saying to the few people that would talk to me at the time, 'I am going to be a star one day'."

That ambition was so deeply rooted that it survived the next 24 years. Possibly because of the lack of talent and the lack of ability it was not the most sensible ambition to have. The strength and tenacity of this ambition might not have made an incredible career, but it has made a great story.

One day the teacher walked in to the classroom and told the children that, if there was anyone interested, the school was organising violin lessons. "Would anyone like to study the instrument?"

John and five other children eagerly raised their hands. "Oh dear," the teacher said, "There is only room for five pupils."

It was decided that the places for the violin lessons should be picked on a 'first come first served' basis, and that the first five in the morning, with a letter from their parents agreeing to the tuition, would get to join the violin class.

John rushed home that night and got his mother to dig out the dusty violin from the attic, and arrived back at school, at 7.30am with both the instrument and the required note.

It was later explained to Class Four however, that there had been a slight rule change to the 'first come first served' basis, and that the applications were now to be judged on ability. Sadly John came sixth.

Before leaving Queens Park Junior School, John did his first audition. CBS Records had a factory for manufacturing records five miles outside Aylesbury, in a little village called Aston Clinton. John and his sister Margaret, two years older and who should have known better, (though, when it comes to stardom our hero can be very persuasive) walked to the place in question, stood at the gates and sang to the delivery truck drivers hoping to get discovered. It proved to be an early rejection from the major labels.

To the surprise of no one, John failed his 11-plus exam. This result meant that he would not go to the local Grammar School, which had a reputation for getting pupils into Oxford and Cambridge, but instead would go to the local Secondary Modern School.

CHAPTER
2

The Grange was a much larger place than Otway had been used to. Whereas Queens Park had been a small local single-sex school, there were two thousand children including girls at The Grange.

He had hated primary and infant school, he felt he had been bullied and misunderstood, and to be fair he had. The Grange was a chance to make a fresh start and leave all those old prejudices behind. If you kept yourself to yourself, you could go unnoticed the majority of the time.

He was lucky with The Grange because a lot of the staff and the headmaster were fiercely ambitious. They felt that the 11-plus system was an unfair way of judging ability, and tried to prove this by going into academic competition with the Grammar and High School (something he would use to his advantage later).

Just before John started at The Grange, the school had their first real academic success. Four pupils had gone through their new sixth form and passed 'A'-levels. One of these was John's sister Frances, and for a short while in this place of learning, the name Otway stood for something worthwhile.

The vast majority of the boys chose this point of graduation to go from wearing short trousers to wearing long trousers. Otway and Jeff Potter, another 11-plus failure from Queens Park, were the only ones not to. The fact that he and Potter were the only ones in this school of two thousand who could be accused of having dirty knees, (and Otway's were, though Potter's always seemed to be clean) was an early point of ridicule, as was the fact that he never used his flies whilst visiting the urinal.

Whether it was the short trousers or not, a bond grew between Otway and Potter that would last many years and become a significant influence on John's career. Potter, the son of a retired army Major, was the complete opposite of Otway. He was well spoken, intelligent, brilliant at sports, good looking and generally well liked. It was a strange partnership, but like another partnership Otway had later, in a strange way it worked.

Within the first term of school, Otway had confided in Potter his ambition and belief in stardom. It would appear that even at this formative stage, Jeffery was converted.

To an extent, Otway had ceased his playground renditions of pop songs. This was, according to Otway, because he had become aware that all the pop stars he knew of were older than him. He reckoned that he would be at least 16 before he could achieve the sort of success he was after. "I didn't want to blow it too early and be a child star," he said at the time.

Instead of putting his career to one side and concentrating on his school work, Otway put his mind to getting the sort of experience he felt he would need later in his chosen path.

Fortune occasionally plays a role in this story. One piece of good luck for the boy was the form teacher assigned to the class for his first two years at the school.

Miss Williams was straight out of training and had the sort of ambition and enthusiasm for the job that inevitably gets knocked out of teachers within two years. Unfortunately for Miss Williams, John instinctively understood ambition and enthusiasm and decided he would do all he could to help teacher.

Most secondary school teachers would agree that the greatest and most disillusioning problem they have with children is apathy. Otway was not a child with this problem.

Up to now teachers had treated Otway only marginally better than his fellow pupils, and John knew that if he was to make his mark in the school, he would need an ally. Miss Williams knew that if she was to make her mark in the school, her form needed to be noticed. Otway was already adept at being noticed, and was more than willing to help out.

One of the first ideas Miss Williams had for the form was a regular bi-weekly magazine. The class she had was 1 Alpha 11 and the publication was to be called the *Alpha-Mail*.

Otway vividly recalls his form mistress explaining that a copy of every magazine and periodical published in Great Britain was sent to, and kept, by the British Library. Perhaps realising that any contribution he managed to get accepted for publication would be kept for prosperity, and available for future Otway historians, he managed to engulf poor Miss Williams with a constant stream of literary output.

The *Alpha-Mail* was printed on the school's spirit duplicator and was neatly hand-written by the teacher herself. However, one edition of the magazine has a poem handwritten by the poet Otway. It was an epic four-pager based on the fairy-tale *Rumpelstiltskin*. Seemingly Miss Williams had taken one look at the mass of paper in John's hand and said: "If you want that to go in you'll have to write it out yourself."

The pages of poem when published were almost illegible. After picking out the line, 'I have been doing some thinking, and wonder if it's Rumplestiltskin,' a historian in the British Library would probably think it lucky that John's writing was so bad.

In the first year the pupils were again offered the opportunity to learn the violin, an offer that John was at last allowed to take up. Tony Freeth used to visit the school once a week to give lessons to those children interested in taking up the instrument.

He liked John. The sort of enthusiasm that was going down so badly elsewhere, somehow seemed to be a breath of fresh air. His encouragement was repaid with a dedication and fanaticism rarely seen in his pupils. John, for that first year, was always seen with a violin. He practiced for many hours a night, got everyone he knew to call him Yehudi, and for the first couple of months to the amazement of everyone made rapid progress.

For this brief period John could share with his mother her love of classical music and the landlord of the local public house increased his takings dramatically as the inhabitants of the household escaped his nightly practice.

It was his first bit of genuine success and everyone was pleased that he had found at least one thing at which he could fare as well as his fellow man. He was shortly in the Junior Orchestra, followed by the Aylesbury Youth Orchestra in which he would remain for the next six years.

John's early problems of physical uncoordination coupled with his inability to play in tune and lack of talent, finally caught up with him after a few months of learning the violin. The determination and hours of practice that had taken him soaring beyond his peers was not enough. Slowly, despite the extra effort, he was caught up and surpassed.

This effort with the violin had not been in vain though. He had got into the orchestra, and his perseverance with the instrument helped a couple of years later when he got his first guitar.

By the second year, John had found a lot of advantage in the greater facilities of this larger school. Schools of that size have things kicking around in cupboards that have long since been forgotten, and it only took the willingness to impress teacher by tidying up the classroom, for Otway to discover a movie camera left by some long-gone film society.

With the briefest glance at this dusty item, our potential star realised he had the opportunity to make a film. Otway and his convert Potter spent the days following the discovery writing scripts, checking locations and planning a suitable way of approaching Miss Williams with the idea of a form film.

With Otway's determination and Potter's encouragement, they attempted to put together a strong enough argument and enough ideas to convince their form mistress.

"Yes," she said, "Why not? The facilities are there and the class could learn a lot from writing a script, choosing a cast and making a film." Not quite what our would-be film makers had in mind.

When 2 Alpha 11 came to choose a star, it was of course Barry Dowdall, the centre forward of the football team. When it came to the script, as so often happens in Hollywood, all the re-writes meant that Otway's only appearance was in the chase scene at the end of the film with the rest of the form. He did as always try and draw as much attention to himself as he could, but his screen début in *No Cups for Thieves* was, even for Otway, a bit of a disappointment.

By the third year John had become frustrated with this lack of attention to his star quality. He and Potter got together, and with a bit of help from his sisters and parents, knocked together a comedy piece about a driving instructor and a farmer. John's family agreed that the finished result was funny enough for a venue larger than the living room and an audience larger than the Otways plus assorted lodgers.

It is here that we find the first example of what was to become almost an Otway trade mark: if he couldn't get a record company to take him, he would start his own and sign himself; if he couldn't find a promoter to put on his shows he would promote himself and give himself star billing; and if he wanted some press exposure and no one would write about him he would start his own magazine or newspaper. This principle would apply to every aspect of his career and was occasionally to prove successful, though most often financially disastrous. What better way to start this trend than devising, arranging, and winning his own talent contest?

Among the entrants to this contest was a pop group called Just Us, run on basic Fascist principles by Warren Harry. Warren's father was the editor of the leading local paper the *Bucks Herald*. Partly by means of his father's influence, and partly because at their time they were a good local band, they worked semi-professionally in the Aylesbury area and achieved considerable local fame.

The talent contest was held at The Grange for the First, Second and Third years, and ended up a battle between Otway and Potter and Just Us. The reason for this was simply that no one apart from the duo took the event particularly seriously, and Just Us were doing what they did every night.

In the end Otway and Potter won. For some reason, which Otway refuses to go into, Just Us were disqualified because they were professionals.

The most astonishing event of that whole year was John coming top of the class in mathematics.

"Yes, that was a bit of a shock for me too," says John now. "All through my life I had been treated like a half-wit, and even I sometimes suspected I might have something wrong up here. Getting that result boosted my self confidence a lot."

CHAPTER
3

It is now that we see a complete change in our hero. The change was inward and philosophical, but the externalisation of this change would be slow and dramatic, not reaching its climax for a further 10 years.

Being top of the class in maths was not just an indication to Otway that he was not a complete idiot, he took it as an early indication of his genius. When starting school for that fourth year he had figured out that up until this point in his life he had been misunderstood. He read the biographies of famous people like Gallileo and Van Gogh and discovered that in their lives too there was ample evidence of misunderstanding and ridicule.

"Yes," he thought to himself, "I am special. The hard time I have suffered is the necessary pain an artist must suffer to create work of artistic merit." And remembering the first time he had felt star-struck all those years ago in Queens Park playground, he felt certain that now he was ready to make the first steps towards the fame and success he craved.

Since starting school at the age of five, John had never really known happiness – he was a loner and the centre of ridicule and abuse. Now he had worked out why this was, it no longer bothered him; in fact he now felt it to be a positive influence and further proof of his talent. He would never again feel sorry for himself, and his optimism and faith in himself would carry him over the many difficulties he would encounter. In short he went from being an ugly duckling to a scruffy awkward duck with a big grin on its face.

The first big problem John had to contend with was getting a guitar. For most people this would not have been a major hurdle, but in his case it was. Mrs Otway by now had some sort of inclination of what was going on in her son's mind, and the years since *Pick of the Pops* had not in any way diminished her hatred of pop music. And there was another problem: Willy Barrett.

As we discovered earlier, Willy lived just up the road from the Otways. By now he had grown his blonde hair to his shoulders and left school at the earliest opportunity. Willy also had musical ambitions, but for far more realistic reasons than John. His father had started teaching him music at the age of four and Willy was a naturally gifted player. Just having left school, and not wanting to get a 'proper job', most of his days were spent wandering up and down Wendover Road with his guitar slung over his shoulder.

"If you get a guitar you're going to grow up like Willy Barrett," his mother would frequently tell him. "You're not getting one and that's final."

Final was not a word that John with his new found confidence understood. He managed to buy an acoustic guitar for £2.50 and a fishing rod (left by an old lodger in the shed), took it home (on the pretext that he was looking after it for a friend), and with a certain deviousness managed to keep the story going for about six months. By this time it was too late. John had learned the six chords he knows today, and was already trying to entertain friends with it.

"I remember that guitar so well," says Otway. "I was so frightened that my mother was going to take it away from me, that I actually slept with it for the first few weeks."

Back at school the new Otway was up to his old tricks of showing off, putting his notoriety down to the fact that he was enigmatic. He would do literally anything as long as it had an audience. It was around this time that the aforementioned ink drinking stunt took place, but there were many other incidents of a similar nature.

Having learned to fight out of necessity, and knowing that playground fights always attracted crowds, Otway would pick fights with all the biggest bullies in the school. Not only that, he would spend a few days before that advertising the event. "That Parker is getting too big for his boots," Otway would say, "I think I should sort him out." "But you'll get totally pummelled," they would sensibly reply. "Just watch me," returned Otway. And they did just that – watch Otway get totally pummelled.

A few hundred yards from the school there is an old foot-bridge crossing the canal and Otway would take a bunch of kids down to watch his display of 'acrobatics'. A description of these is best left to someone who remembers them well: "Bloody hell! That guy used to almost kill himself. It wasn't like he knew what he was doing 'cause he was so awkward, but he'd be doing things like tightrope walking across the handrail, pretend to fall off and leave himself hanging by one foot upside down 30 foot above a solid concrete pavement. Then he'd swing his whole body backwards and forwards and grab the railings, just as his foot came loose. It really was damned scary. The girls used to scream and cry and say to us, 'Get him to stop it,' but we didn't 'cause it was fascinating. In the end the girls stopped coming. I know it sounds stupid now but we used to encourage him to do more and more dangerous things."

Another incident was the circulation of a naked full-frontal photograph of John around the whole school. It was one of the rare occasions that publicity shocked and embarrassed him.

Whilst on a weekend course with a bunch of other kids from the school, John had managed to aggravate his mates to the extent that they felt he should be taught a lesson. One night they waited until he had fallen asleep, ripped the bedclothes away and took the photograph in question. The photo eventually reached the eyes of his sister Margaret, ever protective of her brother, who was so incensed by this shot of her 'Little Rupert' in his birthday suit that she informed the powers-that-be in the school.

The photo did an enormous amount for Otway's notoriety, as it had been so widely circulated. When you think that for some unfortunate young girls this was their first introduction to the male form, you can understand why the photographer, Stephen Pomfrey, was caned and the picture and negatives destroyed by the headmaster.

It is a shame though that we can't print the photo here, as it graphically illustrated both why he got the nickname 'Tiny', and why no member of the fairer sex was interested in him at the time.

Around this time Otway had started to get a few 'friends'. A couple of them were like Potter who believed in John's genius and dreams for the future. The rest were people who discovered that when with Otway, excitement and fun were never far away.

"I bet there are some eggs in that crows nest in those twigs at the top of that very tall tree," one would say, and off he would climb to investigate. "I've just built this raft out of a couple of oil drums and don't know if it will float with someone on it," another would mention. "It doesn't," a drenched Otway would reply, wading back from the middle of a stagnant pond.

This is the boy who was now learning what he could do with the six chords he had mastered on the guitar. Tuning the instrument was, and always would be, a problem for Otway. He got around this at first by taking his guitar to school every day and getting one of Just Us to tune it for him. Sometimes one of them would be kind enough to show him a song or two. As with the violin, he learned rapidly at first, until after a couple of months he became as competent as he is today.

Now he was a guitarist, John believed the time was ripe to form his first group. He approached the other musicians in his year. "But John, Pete Aspley has already formed a group and they are doing their first show at a party next week," one of them told him.

Otway was hurt, and although not particularly jealous by nature, at that party he was. There was Consortium, Pete Aspley's new band, doing exactly what John had been dreaming of doing all these years. And Pete, always a very popular boy with everyone, was the new school pop star.

Otway tried to form a group, but all he could find were people like Potter whose musical ability amounted to zero. He also tried to join Consortium, unsuccessfully apart from one incident.

Always on the look out for opportunities, John spotted in the local paper that a club was running auditions for a TV programme, *Opportunity Knocks*. The winner of this contest would be sponsored by the club as an entrant for the TV show. Otway entered his band and then set about persuading the members of Consortium to join him on this bid for television stardom.

Surprisingly they agreed, but when it came to the night they all decided that, as he had more experience than John, Pete Aspley should do the singing and John should content himself with rhythm guitar. "Things could be worse," thought Otway, "And at least I am in a band."

Throughout that performance he rocked and rolled and looked delighted at his first proper gig. Shortly afterwards however, someone explained to him that the group had unplugged his guitar at the start of the song, and were more than a little amused at his enthusiastic playing.

The hurt of all this was compounded considerably when John, speaking to his mother about his wish to get a band, was told: "John, why do you always want to do what the other kids are doing? Just because Pete Aspley's got a group and is doing well you feel that you have to copy. Why don't you think of something original to do?"

Margaret had just brought a copy of 'Bob Dylan's Greatest Hits' into the Otway household and John fell in love with the record instantly. He felt an affinity with the singer his mother called "The man with the awful voice". Otway, as we can recall from the days of the *Alpha-Mail*, had an interest in poetry and his admiration for Dylan was to continue and be a great source of inspiration to him. Dylan taught Otway that he did not need a band to become a Pop Star, he could do it on his own.

John immediately learnt all the Bob Dylan songs he could, and with a couple of standards like 'Where Do You Go To My Lovely' and 'House Of The Rising Sun', he promoted his first solo appearance at school one lunchtime.

"It was a bit boring," says Otway now, "And the few kids who turned up left after a couple of songs. I hadn't really mastered the art of singing in tune then, which coupled with the guitar tuning being a bit dodgy probably didn't make it sound that good."

In the middle of the fifth year at school, the Aylesbury District Council decided that they would like to widen Wendover Road for a new gyratory system, major road-workings that would demolish the Otway home. So the family had to move, and for better or for worse, they moved into a cul-de-sac called Ash Grove, three doors away from his friend Jeff Potter. This event strengthened the ties between the two and Ash Grove for a while became the headquarters of the Otway career.

It was a useful move in other ways too. Number six, Ash Grove actually backed on to The Grange School, and within a week, John had constructed a bridge over the fence into the school grounds.

'O'-level exams come at the end of the fifth year, and it is with these exams that we see the last reasonable attempt by John to achieve any sort of academic success. He had managed until now to remain top of the class in mathematics, and encouraged by this was able to do fairly well in a few other subjects. When the results were published in the *Bucks Herald*, J. Otway had five 'O'-levels: maths, statistics, physics, history and music.

His parents were delighted. He had done as well as any of his sisters, and it looked as though this son of theirs, who had been such a problem, would eventually be able to hold down a job and become a useful member of society.

One performance that summer was to dash any such hopes that Mr and Mrs Otway might have of their son becoming a useful member of society. Like the scene in the film *The Glenn Miller Story*, where Glenn rushes around saying "The sound, the sound, I have found the sound"; like Archimedes running around the streets naked yelling "Eureka"; Otway was to make his own discovery, his unique and special 'talent'.

CHAPTER 4

The Aylesbury Youth Orchestra held short residential courses during some school holidays. Otway went to one of these at Green Park a few miles outside the town. The orchestra would spend the days on the course learning a symphony or concerto, then give a performance of the piece to an audience of parents, friends and interested people at the end.

There was a fairly rigorous timetable of rehearsals during the day. In the evenings, various entertainments were provided with visiting speakers or performers. One of these evenings was set aside for an informal concert, where groups or individual members of the orchestra could get up and entertain. Often groups would form string quartets and play a little chamber music, others would do solo pieces on whatever instrument they played. It was an informal concert though and basically anything was OK.

It was an opportunity for John to do something, but what? He had discovered that his Bob Dylan repertoire hardly went down a storm, so he thought he would try and do something a little more dramatic. After toying with various ideas, he decided to try and sing 'Where Do You Go To My Lovely', add as much drama and emotion as he could, and use the 'Yelling Voice' he had tried at Queens Park playground. Basically, he thought, "I'll just get up there, sing this song and go completely over the top."

John's performance that night followed some chamber music and an oboe solo. The audience was quiet and politely applauded our young star as he walked on the stage and hammered out the first few chords of the song.

After the first line of singing, a couple of the younger members started giggling with embarrassment, to be joined very shortly by several more. As he hit the first chorus and the first high note of the song, which meant screwing up his face into a contorted shape and forcing all the air in his lungs through his vocal chords as fast as possible, the whole audience erupted. Tears streamed down the faces of that orchestra and one woodwind player actually fell off his chair clutching his sides.

Otway got his first ever standing ovation that night. No one had ever seen anything quite so ridiculous and funny on one of these courses. "I loved that silly singing you did," they said afterwards to a beaming Otway. Even Tony Freeth, who was organiser and conductor, thanked John for a very entertaining piece.

A few weeks after this, John went on another residential course. This time it was for the County Youth Orchestra for players all over Buckinghamshire. As at Green Park there was another informal concert and throughout the week youths from the Aylesbury Orchestra kept asking John if he would be doing his silly singing at this event. As we well know he needed no encouragement, and this time the Aylesbury contingent of that audience cheered him as he took the stage.

Another thing of great import occurred during that course. Among the audience of that performance was an attractive young viola player, Sue Reece. Whether or not she was terribly impressed with the performance is not certain, but John was to fall in love with her instantly and she would be his sweetheart for the next two years. From this stage onwards, love and romance would play a huge role in the Otway story. It would be the one thing that could ever distract him from his chosen path.

One day whilst reading the Musicians Wanted section of *Melody Maker*, John noticed an advert, 'Fiddle player wanted for folk duo', with an Aylesbury phone number. Obviously an immediate call was in order, and soon, violin in hand, John was off to the other side of the town to meet Dave Zampy.

Dave was a folk singer. There were many of them around 1968, playing the numerous folk clubs that were blossoming in small halls up and down the country. Dave Zampy played Leonard Cohen, Incredible String Band and Donovan sort of things. To give his act a little bit of an edge Dave felt it would be a neat idea to add a fiddle player. The two of them got together, worked out a few numbers, and went to try their luck in the clubs. Over the next few weeks or so, they played several of these places going down reasonably well in the three-number floor spot they were given.

At this time Willy Barrett appears on the scene yet again, starting his own folk club above a pub called The Derby Arms.

His new club was to be called The Bog Hog and Dave and John went to meet him to see if they could play on the opening night.

It should be mentioned at this point that Willy had achieved considerable fame in and around Aylesbury, and no one would dispute the fact that he was the most accomplished guitarist in the area. He played and had a love of early blues and American bluegrass music. He also played fiddle, banjo and steel guitar brilliantly. He was at the time making a good living from a whole circuit of folk clubs which he topped up with winnings from games of three-card brag in The Derby Arms.

John had heard a lot about Willy, everyone had, but he had not spoken to him since the age of seven and had never seen him play. Dave and John went up to the pub to meet him and play him a song.

Although John knew that Willy played violin, he reckoned that, as it was only his second instrument, and John had been practising an hour and a half every night for five years, he could teach Willy a thing or two about the instrument. He showed off his playing to Willy as he backed Dave's song and then handed the fiddle to Willy with a sort of "OK, big star, show us what you can do" gesture. Willy did show John exactly what he could do, making John's attempt sound totally amateurish. And he had to buy Willy a pint of lager as the pub burst into spontaneous applause. Willy thought what Dave and John were doing was alright and, as they were quite willing to do their three numbers for nothing, agreed to let them play at the club.

That first night at The Bog Hog was packed, and John felt that as well as a couple of violin numbers with Dave, he should attempt to do 'Where Do You Go To' in the same manner as he had at the music courses.

The reaction to that performance was pretty similar to the previous ones. However, quite a few of the audience thought that it was horrendous and headed straight downstairs to the bar as soon as he started singing. A good half stayed though and gave him yet another standing ovation.

Dave Zampy was not at all pleased. He was struggling to make a name for himself as a serious performer, and having this nutter doing a circus routine in the middle of the act did a lot to destroy any credibility he was building up. After a few similar occasions, Dave Zampy was to decide that working with Otway was professional suicide and they split up.

The following week and the week after that, Otway turned up to The Bog Hog to sing 'Where Do You Go To'. After four weeks of the same song, Willy finally asked John whether he knew any others. "Not that I can do like that," he replied, walking on stage to do it yet again. Willy told John that if he wanted to play there again he would need a repertoire larger than one song.

For the next few weeks (actually it turned out to be the next few years), John would drive his family, especially his mother, around the bend as he found new songs that he could do with his 'silly singing'. Having only an eight note range to his voice, finding material was difficult for him, so he started writing his own.

Before we discuss these first serious attempts at writing, let's look at the other things that were going on in his life, for these are the influences that were surrounding our young artist and would affect his creative output.

The sixth form at The Grange was very different from the earlier years. There was far more freedom, as one only had to attend the lessons one needed for the 'A'-levels two years later.

At the Grammar School one was allowed to study a maximum of three 'A'-levels. Otway worked out that should he be able to get four he would be regarded as some sort of academic hero. With this in mind he put his name down to study pure maths, applied maths, statistics and physics. Because of the competition between The Grange and the Grammar School, the school was quite happy to go along with this idea. They foolishly imagined that because he had put his name down for these subjects, he was going to work hard and do his best to get them. Had he done so he would have become the only scholar in the town to pass this many exams.

Having discovered his ability to win audiences, school work soon became the least important element in his life. He found uses for that place of learning that were far more educational in terms of his career than maths lessons.

After his success at 'O'-levels, John was rewarded for his effort at school by being made a school prefect. This position was used by the staff to cut down their work load, and loved only by those pupils who were Fascist by nature, and enjoyed disciplining the younger members of the school. Otway, however, discovered it was a way to increase his popularity and build an audience.

Using the formula that children eventually grow into adults and are more easily converted whilst young, John embarked on a process of indoctrination. He noted the fact that the prefects, apart from giving lines and keeping them out of the school at lunchtimes, had nothing at all to do with the pupils in the first years at The Grange. Bearing this in mind, he spent that first term walking around the school saying "Good

Morning" to all the first year girls. He would get to know their names and, when on door duty, he would make decoys for the other prefects so that the young girls could sneak into the school out of the cold.

It worked brilliantly, and soon all the girls in that year knew his name, spoke to him, and thought "what a nice prefect." It was now time to put all that effort to use.

Otway approached the music teacher with the idea of giving a folk concert in the music room one lunchtime. Having got that sorted out, he went to the art department and persuaded the arts' master to do a project that involved making posters for the event. For the next two weeks, Otway was seen around the playground telling his first year girls that they must come and see him sing.

To make sure that everyone knew that this event was taking place, he also made use of the school Tannoy system. The Grange had a loudspeaker system in each classroom and the headmaster would announce messages at five to 12 each school-day. On the day in question, Mr Dorrance announced that John Otway would be giving a folk concert in the music room that lunchtime.

The audience at that concert consisted of Potter and a couple of other people his age who had come to see what Otway was up to now, Mr Pillinger the Music teacher, and about 80 first year girls. It was John's first full-length concert in his new style.

Luckily the music department had a tape recorder, and a recording still exists of this event, so we know for certain that Otway is not exaggerating when he says it went down a storm. Listening to the tape it is almost impossible to work out what on earth he is doing. First there are a couple of guitar strums, followed by Otway yelling a couple of lines, followed by a barrage of screams, yes screams, from the throats of four score of 12-year-old girls.

By now, Otway had discovered 'Silly Singing' was not effective enough on its own. It sounded horrible, it was out of tune, and though at first amusing, a whole show of it was more than even his first year fans could take. To get around this problem John started adding a wild theatrical side to the show. As soon as he felt the singing was starting to pall on the audience he would spontaneously do something to continue the attention.

He would crawl around the floor, burst into tears, waddle around the stage with his guitar between his legs, rip his shirt open and do things with his body that for someone more coordinated than Otway would have been impossible.

The sight of a sixth form prefect acting in this way had a predictable effect on these impressionable young ladies and he became a bit of a hero/mascot.

Having discovered a new more constructive way of attracting attention, John's other 'High Profile' playground and bridge antics became history. They became historic with a well-remembered final playground climax, which happened in his last years in that school.

Steve Easton was two years younger than Otway, but he was tough. He and his brother Gary had the effect on the school that the Kray brothers had on the East End of London. Everyone was frightened of Steve, who had the constant air of someone not to mess with.

By the time Otway heard his name, he had already attacked a number of staff, and the area behind the cycle sheds (where he and his gang went for a fag) had become a no-go area as far as the authorities were concerned.

It must be emphasised at this point that the paths of Otway and Easton had never crossed. John, for his part, was happy cultivating his young female fans, while Easton was quite happy building up a minor equivalent of the Mafia.

Otway and Potter discussed this new phenomenon. They saw parallels between thirties Chicago and sixties Grange School. Potter, on Otway's behalf decided Otway should take the role of Elliot Ness in *The Untouchables*.

Potter felt very strongly that should Otway manage to beat up Easton and crush his stranglehold on the school, he would not only be doing the place a favour, he would also make himself a hero. Otway was not as convinced as Potter, dealing with someone like Easton could be described as possibly suicidal and at best painful.

"But look, if you manage to beat him up you'll be a real hero," Potter explained over and over again. John was very susceptible to the idea of being a real hero, but the stakes were high and it took Potter a whole week of endless persuasion to get him to agree to do it.

Once agreed, Potter made sure John could not back out of the deal by advertising the forthcoming bout around the school for two days. And so the scene was set for Otway's final playground epic.

On this particular occasion, John had no problem assembling an audience to come and watch. This lunchtime he strode across the playground towards the no-go area with Potter and spectators a safe distance behind.

It was the surprise element. If Easton had noticed Otway in the past he would certainly not have thought of him as any sort of threat: as Otway entered his area he probably thought he was someone after a fag. He must have been taken aback when John started hitting him. In fact, it took him so long to work out what was happening that his nose was bleeding before he had raised his fists to fight back. By this time the Otway retreat had started as he carefully moved backwards to safer ground.

To be fair to Otway he had put up a good fight, and to be fair to Easton he was taken completely by surprise. By the time the staff arrived to break up the fight, the amount of blood coming out of Easton's nose indicated that Otway had won, though hardly by the Queensbury rules.

There is an appendix to this story. Dave Fountain, the head boy, chairing a prefects' meeting and discussing the Easton problem later, said, "Look, if Otway can beat the guy up, then anyone can." He was wrong. The next day Dave Fountain had to visit the Royal Bucks Hospital out-patients after a brief visit to the no-go area.

After the Easton fight, Otway's fearlessness came to the attention of Tony Redman, the sports master in charge of the school rugby team.

"Why don't you join the team for a match, Otway?" Mr Redman asked. "You haven't had the chance to represent the school on the sports field, have you?"

It was quite true, he hadn't. "I'd love to" said Otway delighted, remembering how popular with the girls the boys in the sports teams were.

Mr Redman had one very frightened rugby team. The match coming up was against Mandeville School. Mandeville rugby team consisted of the biggest bunch of thugs ever to grace a pitch in Aylesbury, and every member of that team dwarfed every member of The Grange team. In their previous matches, after the first few bruises, members of The Grange team had virtually gift wrapped the ball and presented it to the opposition. Mr Redman needed someone to show courage. Being one of the members of staff who broke up the Easton fight, he thought John could be the player his team was missing.

John of course had no sports kit whatsoever. For that match he graced the pitch in his black lace-up school shoes, odd socks and a pair of shorts borrowed from someone a great deal tubbier than himself.

There was good and bad news for Mr Redman in that match against Mandeville. The good news: Otway fearlessly hurled himself at the legs of any member of the opposition he could, stopping them in their tracks and sending them crashing to the floor. The bad news: having done that, and gained possession of the ball, he would invariably present it to the opposition. This was not intentional. His lack of coordination meant that he sent the ball in the wrong direction should he either throw or kick it.

The final result was exactly the same as it would have been had John not played, Mandeville 40 Grange 0.

Jeff Potter had a sister Liz, a couple of years younger than himself. She was a pretty girl, to whom Otway had sent his first Valentine card at the age of nine. Unlike Jeff, she had passed her 11-plus and went to the girls' High School. Around this time, she started dating a rather greasy, shady, entrepreneurial character called Chris France.

Chris went to the boys' Grammar School. He had decided to rectify the lack of physical contact between the members of the two schools by organising ballroom dancing lessons, and making sure that the last thing anyone learned at them was ballroom dancing.

When Otway and France met, Chris was a sight! He wore his Grammar School uniform with huge bell-bottom trousers, eight-inch platform shoes and black lank shiny hair down to his shoulders.

Chris also had a 'car' – a nine-year-old Austin A40 which he had painted in psychedelic colours. Chris was intrigued by Otway and Potter. Shortly the duo became a trio and Liz saw less and less of Chris as he started spending more and more time at The Derby Arms with Otway and Potter.

The HQ of the Otway career had now pretty much moved to The Derby Arms. The landlord Ted was pretty lenient about who he allowed to drink there, so it was a public house with a large number of undesirables. Few were more undesirable than Otway, Potter and France, though one possible exception was Willy Barrett.

Otway, as we shall discover over and over again, was a disaster with money. Chris was more sensible. (Actually 'sensible' is completely the wrong word for Chris' dealings with money, but because no word in the English language exists to describe his financial dealings, sensible will have to do.) He would become, and still is, Otway's personal banker and loan shark.

Because of his rather dubious sense of adventure, he has remained one of Otway's closest friends, and is probably right when he says, "I suppose life would have been a lot duller if I had not met Otway."

The Derby Arms and the blossoming music scene in Aylesbury also introduced John to several other interesting characters.

One of these was Kris Needs, a lover of the new progressive music. His own brand of insanity attracted him to Otway and his show. Kris Needs was drawing psychedelic illustrations for a few places, including a new club called Friars in the town, and wanted to be involved with music in any way he could. Having seen and fallen in love with Tyrannosaurus Rex, he bought himself a pair of bongo drums and painted them psychedelic colours. He and John then agreed to do what Marc Bolan had done and form a duo.

What Kris and John had in common was a lack of style made up for by an excess of enthusiasm. Kris Needs could effect an incredible blood-curdling scream, and his idea of how good a gig was was measured by how much blood came out of his fingers at the end of a bongo solo. These were the sort of qualifications John felt he needed in a partner, and the two of them were to work together for over a year.

In July every year in Aylesbury there is a carnival. In July 1970, the climax of the day was to be an open air music concert in the Market Square, featuring local groups. This part of the festivities was called Hobble On The Cobbles. The acts appearing that night were picked by Dave James, a local DJ and dance promoter, who had a regular pop column in the *Bucks Herald*. When these acts were announced in his column, Otway's name was notable by its absence.

Being the biggest event in the town that year, Otway badly wanted to play. But how? Outside The Grange and The Derby Arms he was not yet well known. Even John knew that auditioning for Dave James or inviting him down to The Bog Hog would guarantee that he would not be included on the bill. Would the organisers of this event allow Otway to take the stage without the faintest idea of what he would do when he took it?

In the end, John devised a plan to present Dave James with a petition from his thousands of fans in the town, insisting that the night would not be the same if he didn't play. It was so obvious that the night would not be the same without him that getting people to sign proved no problem.

For the next week John toured The Grange playground getting signatures. His first year girls took the petition around the whole of their year, The Bog Hog crowd added theirs, and by fair means or foul, by the time the document was ready for presentation, it was six-feet long and contained two thousand signatures. There were a few signatures of people Otway was unlikely to know, like Mickey Mouse, Batman and Robin and Harold Wilson, but these probable forgeries were outnumbered by the real thing.

John posted the petition anonymously, with his name, address and phone number on the envelope so Dave James would know how to contact him. Sure enough, two days later,

Dave phoned Otway to find out what he played, and why, with him having so many fans in the town, he hadn't heard of him.

"It's folk music I do," said Otway. "I play a lot at Willy Barrett's folk club and other places like that".

"Oh," replied Dave, "I know Willy, he's a really good player. If you're like him it should be OK."

Dave went on to explain that the petition would make a good story in his pop column, emphasizing how important the artistes in the area considered the event to be.

Otway had done it! To his delight, he saw his name in the paper among the various local luminaries due to appear.

For the week preceding this performance, John was a nervous wreck. He gave up smoking to improve his singing, and could talk of nothing else but the forthcoming event.

The day arrived, and the local populace of Buckinghamshire's County Town lined the pavements to watch the floats in the carnival, then gathered in the Market Square to watch the bands.

Otway and Kris were allowed four numbers, and decided to go all out and do the wildest they could. As soon as they started, Dave James discovered to his horror something that John knew all along. He was nothing at all like Willy. After his second number, an angry Mr James came on stage and firmly told Otway to do only one more.

His final song, which was a lengthy adaption of a poem called 'The Highwayman', was the song in which Otway ripped his shirt open and Kris made his fingers bleed and did The Scream. Dave's fine sense of musical taste was so offended by all of this that he walked on stage three times during the number to ask if it was over yet. It wasn't too bad as far as early Otway shows went. Someone later described it as "Having the same fascination as an aeroplane disaster."

In the Market Square that evening was Steve Peacock, a young reporter from *Sounds*, the national music paper. He had been sent to review a performance by Lol Coxhill, a pretty famous saxophone player. Steve liked Otway's manic performance and decided to write about it in the piece he was doing.

"When I was told I had a review in *Sounds*," Otway explains, "I went tearing up the town with Potter to get a copy. I really embarrassed him. I kept leaping up and down in W.H.Smiths yelling 'Yeah, yeah, I've made it, I've made it, I've been discovered,' and bought all 20 copies in the shop."

Before going too deeply into John's reaction to this short review, it is worth printing in full the first introduction the world at large had to our hero: "The surprise and amazement of the evening though was a short but overpowering set by a guy called John Otway, who sang and hammered inaudible guitar, while his sidekick Kris hammered bongos until I thought his fingers would drop off in a bloody pulp. Words just haven't been devised to deal with a performance like John Otway's – he sings so badly (in a conventional sense) with such conviction and performs with such a natural sense of theatre that he is totally riveting."

Otway really did believe he had made it. A review in a national organ of the music press in the UK was, he thought, overnight success.

"You must bear in mind", he says, "That I didn't know anyone else who had national coverage for their show, so I thought I'd really hit the big time."

The next month Otway posted copies of the review off to the most unlikely places. The BBC TV centre got a copy, with the suggestion that they send someone down to The Bog Hog to see him play, so did BBC radio. He thought it might get him a job doing his show on boats, so he sent one to P & O. And, after reading in *Melody Maker* that acts were wanted for clubs in Holland, a *Sounds* review was sent abroad.

John's mum even made the suggestion that several people had been discovered working as Redcoats at Butlins, and if John felt he hadn't been discovered enough, maybe he should send them one.

It would take John a while to realise that what he originally thought was overnight success was in fact only a small step in the right direction.

CHAPTER 6

s the following Christmas arrived, so did the annual Red Cross Bazaar. Mr and Mrs Otway helped raise funds by selling the potted plants John's dad grew in the greenhouse. Another fund raiser was Mrs Clerk, who read fortunes with cards and a crystal ball. What should have been taken as a bit of fun was taken by Otway to be Gospel and his destiny.

She gazed into her crystal ball: "I can see a golden bird, I think it is a symbol of great wealth and fame." As she read the cards she added, "I can see you playing to crowds all over the world with a blonde-haired musician. It will take some time to achieve success, with a lot of ups and downs, but your first big break will come when there is snow on the ground."

Otway was ecstatic. The repercussions of that visit were to be many, as he now felt 'chosen'. It was his fate and destiny to be a star and the 50p to the Red Cross for the reading was the best 10 bob he'd ever donated in his life.

The lyrics of the song 'Gypsy' probably say more about the faith John had in Mrs Clerk's predictions than anything else:

> In her hands I take another day
> In her breast I hear her heart
> I will wait until tomorrow
> Then I'll smile and say she's right
> Then smile on and laugh about it
> I see a golden bird
> Spreading wings that you might fly
> Underneath a stardust sky
> And never ask why
> But understand.

The only blonde-haired musician that John could think of was Willy Barrett. It was a complete long-shot that Willy would work with him, but if it was fate, then it was worth a go. He called Willy and enthusiastically explained his sure-fire bid for stardom. Willy agreed to come over and have a jam.

Having a jam with Otway meant spending two hours watching John trying to tune a guitar.

"I was a bit embarrassed about asking Willy to tune my guitar for me," says John, "So I kept trying to tune it myself. Every time I thought I'd got it about right I'd look up and Willy would be shaking his head". In the end, Willy tuned John's guitar and for the remaining 30 minutes they played a couple of things.

John had a gig coming up at the Aylesbury College of Further Education, supporting a band called Trees, so he suggested to Willy that they should do it together.

"I'll go on and warm them up with a couple of numbers on my own," said John, "Then you can do a couple, and we'll do some together at the end." That agreed they organised a couple of rehearsals for the big day.

It would be the first gig for the hit-duo-to-be. In later years they would get considerable publicity for the amount of times they split up. On this occasion they actually split up before they got together.

Otway was terribly nervous at the thought of playing with Willy. He hadn't done many big gigs with microphones and he was really tense. In situations like these, any trace of restraint became non-existent. For his entrance for the two solo numbers, he ran on stage like a screaming banshee, having forgotten to get Willy to tune his guitar. It would be years before Otway perfected his microphone technique, and perfect was certainly not a word that could apply to it that night.

A mixture of nerves, stupidity and pints of bitter were a lethal cocktail, and Willy watched horrified as an act he used to find mildly amusing in his folk club became an embarrassing noise. In the end, after most of the audience had left for the bar to escape, the sound-man turned the PA off, leaving Otway yelling acoustically to a half-empty hall.

After John had been removed from the stage, Willy came on to play his numbers, and the place rapidly filled up again to hear the nice acoustic blues playing that Willy was so good at. Predictably he went down well. Angry and heartbroken, Otway watched from the side of the stage, knowing well there was no way that they would play together that night.

As is often the way with inexperienced performers, blame for a bad sound is placed firmly and directly at the feet of the technical crew. The sound system belonged to the headline band, Trees, and John felt that there had been a conspiracy to make him sound bad so that they'd sound good. Otway stormed into their dressing room in the intermission and had a blazing row with the band.

"I didn't deserve a bad sound like that," yelled Otway. "But you were making it," they replied. "My guitar sounded horrible," he screamed. "Of course it did, it was out of tune." "Well why didn't you do something about it?" said Otway at his most ridiculous.

After this gig, Otway and Barrett, by mutual agreement, decided that there must be other blonde-haired musicians around, and Otway went looking.

John had now reached his final year at school and Mrs Otway felt that her family had grown up enough for her to get a job. With both his parents at work all day, the house was empty – John thought that this was a waste of space which he decided to utilise.

As we know, the Otway house backed on to the school and a bridge had been built over the six-foot fence. The more disreputable female elements of the fourth year (three years younger than John) were introduced to the Otway home by Potter. Potter's interest in the fairer sex, and theirs in him, had been going on for some years. Otway's home proved an ideal spot for Jeff to introduce young ladies to the arts of love, as well as being a good place to drink and smoke. So close to, yet so far from, the eyes of authority.

Once Potter had introduced a couple of girls to number six, Ash Grove, more and more of them began to gather. They discovered it was a pretty neat place to go: John was pretty easy going, and they all knew where the key was hidden if they arrived before him. They started bringing their own boyfriends. Kris Needs started coming up from the Grammar School, and a sort of lunchtime club built up.

The place became so popular, and so much fun, that soon lunchtime was not long enough, and it started spreading into the afternoon. As the school year went on, school would start at nine and finish at mid-day. Inevitably, in the end someone at school noticed, and the fun was curtailed to a certain extent. But the damage to everyone's academic progress had already been done.

In order to fund his nicotine and beer habits, John had got himself an early morning job cleaning the school youth club. Anyone who has seen Otway first thing in the morning will know that there is no way at all that he can have been particularly good at it. One story illustrates just how bad he was.

Rather than go to school after cleaning the youth club one day, John decides to go back to bed after a hard morning's work. About half an hour into his slumbers he is woken by two teachers, asking earnestly if he had cleaned the school youth club that morning. "Yes, of course I did", said a worried John, "I did my full hour and a half. I started at seven and finished at half eight." "Well the police are round there and they want to see you."

John was worried. He couldn't imagine, even if he did not do a perfect cleaning job, why the police should be brought in. "If they think I'm not doing it well enough they shouldn't pay me. Bringing in the forces of law and order is a bit heavy." John was met at the youth club by a detective who takes him upstairs.

"Did you clean up here?" he asked John, pointing to the corridor. "Yes, I do that every day." "And you didn't notice this pile of saw-dust on the floor when you were sweeping up?" he asked. "Er... umm... no I didn't. I suppose I should have swept it but I didn't see..." said Otway going red in the face. "I'm surprised" (so is everyone else standing around) "that you didn't notice that, but did you notice this office door that has been pried open with a crowbar and left hanging off its hinges?"

Amazing, or not, John had worked that morning at the scene of an earlier crime and had not even noticed these things, let alone cleaned them up. The police needed to speak to him as he was the first person there after the burglary, but he was of no use to them whatsoever. He unwittingly did what we all should do in the event of discovering such a crime: leave all the evidence intact for the detectives. They did have that to thank him for.

John had continued working with Kris Needs, and his status as the town loony was growing as he used techniques he had learned at The Grange to increase his notoriety.

Friars, a local music club, had been running for about a year in a small ex-servicemen's club. It ran on a Monday night, and had a considerable amount of groups playing there who would be famous later. Among these were Genesis, Free and Mott The Hoople.

Dave Stopps promoted the venue, and rather than simply be a promoter, he ran the place as a genuine club. He did this with such style that it became The Place To Be. Otway, Potter and France certainly went there, and Kris Needs as we mentioned did the psychedelic artwork for the club's newsletter and posters. Before Otway could persuade Dave Stopps to let him play at the club though, the ex-servicemen themselves decided that they had had enough of hippies and closed the club down.

It took Dave Stopps a while to find another venue, and by the time he had, Hobble On The Cobbles had been and gone. Dave had been the recipient of a *Sounds* review with the note "How about a gig at Friars?" attached.

Friars' new venue was the Borough Assembly Hall in Aylesbury, a much larger place that held about 500 people. Dave was lucky with the first show he booked there. The act he put on was The Groundhogs, and the day before they were due to play, they were on *Top Of The Pops*, as their single 'Cherry Red' had just entered the charts. Dave had taken the gamble and put John and Kris on to do a short set before the hit act.

Because of the hit record, and being the first night of the club for a while, the place was packed. John looked out on those people that they were about to play to, and said to Kris, "I want to see a sea of bopping heads," and then repeated it over and over again.

Because he would need amplification for a show of this size, Otway had built an electric pick-up for his guitar, so it could be plugged into an amplifier. It was a bit of a Heath Robinson affair, but it seemed to work OK. That is until he tried it out on stage in front of 500 people.

"Now, that was embarrassing," he says. "The Friars audience were known for being warm and giving acts encouragement, so Dave announced me, and there was all this applause. I hammered the guitar to start the show and no sound came out. But I got it going in the end."

What Otway is failing to tell us here is what "got it going" really meant.

Basically, thumping the front of the guitar with his fist somehow connected two wires inside the instrument, and it worked for a few seconds before needing to be thumped again. As the set went on, the harder and harder he had to thump it. Unfortunately, the guitar was attached to John's trousers, and each time he took a swipe at the guitar his trousers came down a little. Those cognisant with the Otway line in underwear can imagine the effect of all this on the audience, and why he got so much applause when Kris' bongo solo came around and he had the chance to cover them up again. By the time Kris' scream happened, the audience were well won over, and the show turned out to be one of Otway's most successful so far.

John's school days were coming to an end. He had been saying all year that he would revise and do all the work in the last month before the exams. Three weeks into the last month he said he would do all the revision and work in the last week. The day before his first 'A'-level, Otway said to Potter, "Let's go up the pub, 'cause I'm a little worried about the exams".

The Bog Hog, the first year girls, the lunchtimes at home, his romance with Sue Reece, the predictions of Mrs Clerk,

Willy Barrett, Jeff Potter, Chris France and Kris Needs had all taken their toll. The result was inevitable. John failed all four 'A'-levels.

CHAPTER 7

John instinctively knew he had not done well in his 'A'-levels, and he knew he would have to get some sort of job until his career picked up enough for him to go professional. He reckoned he had to work fast and get something good between leaving school and the time the exam results came out.

Unfortunately, this plan did not work too well. Prospective employers were impressed when he told them how many 'O'-levels he had, and even more impressed when he told them how many 'A'-levels he expected to get. There was one thing that did not impress them however. As a referee on his job application form, John put down "The Head Of The Sixth Form, Grange County Secondary School, Aylesbury".

"I just thought it was the right sort of thing one puts on those forms," explains Otway. With most people it probably was the right sort of thing, but if one wanted a job, the last thing one needed was a reference that went something like this:

"John has not spent a great deal of time at school for the last two years. Rather than concentrate on his academic studies, he has concentrated on playing his guitar and giving concerts of Pop Music. He has not been a constructive member of our sixth form, and furthermore, I do not expect him to do at all well in this years' exams."

Poor John could not understand why, when he was doing so well in interviews, he was failing so badly in getting a job.

Eventually he did gain employment, as a trainee quantity surveyor with the Aylesbury Borough Council. After he had been there a while, his boss told him about the reference he'd received.

"I was a bit worried about employing you," he said to him, "But then I thought what a nice lad you were in the interview. I didn't think that reference was the right way for a school to start someone off in their working life, so I thought I'd take the risk and give you the job".

He was probably wrong to give John the job, and will probably get more rewards in heaven for his kind-hearted gesture than he got from Otway as a trainee quantity surveyor.

Otway discovered pretty quickly that he hated work. School hours were short in comparison to work hours, and in comparison to John's school hours, work felt like a prison sentence.

The building trade was not the sort of thing that appealed to John, nor come to that the sort of thing he was at all good at. He was quite good at mathematics because he could understand the concepts of Newton and calculus, but at arithmetic he was useless. He never managed to learn his times tables, but remembers the solution of a quadratic equation to this day. It is why he suddenly shot from around the bottom of the class in maths at school to the top.

Quantity surveying is basically all arithmetic. You receive drawings from an architect, and from them work out how many bricks, how much cement and other materials it would take to build whatever the architect has in mind. On one occasion, from John's calculations, it would have taken an area twice the size of the proposed building to store the left-over bricks and mortar.

"He's the only person I know who can consistently make mistakes with a calculator," a work mate said of him.

It was his times tables that let him down. Within six months, to the benefit of both star and the Aylesbury Borough Council, John left his first real job to go professional. It was a rash move.

Having a job meant Otway had started earning money. Earning money taught him one financial rule that he has applied ever since: the more money you earn, the more you can get into debt. Almost as soon as he received his first wage packet, he started to put this rule into practice.

"Chris, I think I ought to go into a recording studio to record some of my songs. It will cost £100, but now I'm working I would be able to pay you back at a tenner a week if you lent me the money," John said.

And so John got into debt, a state from which he has only once briefly escaped.

Otway knew that in order to go into the studios he would need a good musician. Kris Needs' bongo playing and screams looked good on stage, but they were not the sort of thing hit records were made of. Bearing in mind that Willy was the only blonde musician he knew at all, it was worth another attempt at getting together.

This was not as difficult as it sounded. Willy had done some studio work before, and he had just been on the radio, playing bluegrass music on a late night BBC show. As long as someone else was paying, he was quite willing to get some more experience in the studio, especially since Otway told him he could be the producer.

And so it was that Otway the star, Potter the believer, Chris France the financier and Willy Barrett the musician and producer, headed off to Maidenhead's Pro-Musica studio in Chris' psychedelic Austin A40 one April evening in 1972.

The songs they chose to record were 'Gypsy', John's ode to Mrs Clerk, and 'Misty Mountain', a tune Otway and Barrett had messed about with. It had no words when they began that journey, but luckily had by the time they arrived at Maidenhead.

This was the first time they had worked constructively together. For some strange reason Willy's beautiful acoustic slide playing on 'Gypsy' supported John's singing in a way that made his voice less offensive to the ear, as did his fiddle playing on 'Misty Mountain'. It was a good recording and Willy was pleased with the results.

Otway was ecstatic. "It's going to be really big, isn't it?" he said to Willy. "It's going to be a bloody hit," he said to France. "Hit before Christmas," Otway and Potter said together.

"Hit before Christmas," was a phrase that would crop up every year, even as late as 1987.

After sending the tapes off a few times, Otway, Potter and France were to be disappointed. Otway and Potter because no one was interested in releasing the recording, and Chris France because he never saw the promised tenner a week.

After the recording session, Otway was back in Willy's good books, and Willy started taking John around his circuit of folk clubs. Originally the idea was for Otway to strum the chords behind Willy's fiddle and banjo playing. In return, John would get to play the nice 'Gypsy' song and earn the odd fiver. A good idea in theory, but in practice more and more of the wild Otway crept into Willy's shows. As this wild element increased, Willy's re-bookings decreased proportionately, and after some really extravagant performances, Otway managed to get Willy banned from a couple of places.

Otway still owed Chris France the £100 for the recording, and his final wage packet, which was supposed to get him over the first difficult period, dried up after three days. He was very soon in dire straits.

Chris France's father had bought up a positive mountain of zips from a firm that had gone bankrupt. These zips arrived at the France home in great mixed bales: long ones, short ones, some nylon, some metal and in all different colours. In order to re-sell these zips to market stalls and the like, they all needed sorting out: they had to be re-packed, tagged by size, colour and material. Chris' father had been paying Chris four pounds a hundred to do this work. Chris, seeing Otway in such difficulties, magnanimously offered to help him out by sub-contracting him to do the work at two pounds a hundred.

John thought this was the perfect way of solving his immediate problems and had 10,000 zippers delivered to Ash Grove so he could make some money. And so it was that the Otway home became a zip-packing factory.

Bearing in mind that these zips had to be sorted into piles of colour, length and material, and bearing in mind that Otway was not the tidiest person in the world, you can understand how the carpet and furniture of the complete ground floor of that house came to be covered in zippers. Added to all of this, in the middle of the living room floor John had built an elaborate machine that cut the plastic packing bags to the right length, in order to increase productivity.

Neither Mr nor Mrs Otway particularly enjoyed having the family home turned into an industrial estate, and on the arrival of another 10,000 zips, Jack Otway decided the time had come to have words with his son. The words he chose were along the lines of: "This is ridiculous, either be sensible and get a proper job or find somewhere else to live."

Being sensible was not something our hero was particularly adept at, and so, out of the two options offered to him by his father, he chose the latter. Having packed his bags and picked up a tenner of his wages from Chris France, he left home.

At first an old school-friend, who had sensibly got a flat for himself before leaving home, put him up. But living with Otway is not the easiest thing in the world and the arrangement lasted only a few days.

The difficulty of looking after himself suddenly hit Otway hard. But being a man of great imagination, an idea was not long in coming.

"Willy," John asked "Would it be alright if I lived in your car for a while 'til I get something else sorted out? I mean it would have advantages. You wouldn't have to drive me home after gigs at night."

This arrangement, for obvious reasons, did not last long either. For a long while afterwards, John would feel bitter about being evicted from Barrett's car.

"It was awful," says Otway. "One day he just drove me up to The Derby Arms in my new home, dropped me and my things off and drove away in it."

Luckily Potter was in the pub that night and offered to help get Otway out of the mess he was in. "My mother has got one of these little pup tents, you know, just big enough to get you and a sleeping bag into. If you were really careful with it, I'm sure you could borrow it."

That night a psychedelic A40 dropped John and a small tent off in a beauty spot, called Whiteleaf Cross, in the Chiltern Hills.

"I did feel bad about dropping him off like that," says Chris. "For one thing he was earning me a lot of money doing those zips, and I knew he couldn't work from that tent. Another is that none of us knew how to put the tent up and as we left, John was scrambling around the hillside in the dark trying to find poles and things."

Dark times indeed for our young star, but there were compensations for this suffering. If indeed hard times like these bring out inspiration and creative genius, then it can possibly be seen in the song 'Trying Times' in which Otway describes his ordeal:

> Then the sky turned black and it grew cold and still
> And the western wind blew up the hill
> And the autumn leaves fell sheltering me
> From the cold and dark night that grew around me.

Another compensation lay in the fact that Sue Reece, his girlfriend, lived just down the road from Whiteleaf Cross, in a small village called Monks Risborough. Most mornings after packing his tent, he would carry it down the hill and walk the two miles to Sue's house. After checking that her parents had gone to work, he would hide the tent in the garage and Sue would make him breakfast.

One evening, Mr Reece discovered John retrieving his tent from the garage, and was horrified to discover where his daughter's boyfriend was living. Sue's parents kindly put John up for a couple of weeks on their sofa.

Things could not last like this forever, and eventually Mr Otway agreed that John could come home, on the condition that he got a proper job and that there would not under any circumstances be any more zips.

CHAPTER 8

John's first proper job was in a factory making vinyl folders, his next was as a booking clerk for British Rail. He thought that neither would last, but he had come to realise that it was far easier to go for stardom if you lived somewhere.

Because of the eviction from Willy's car, Otway and Barrett had split up. "Nothing," John said, "Would persuade me to work with him ever again, that is it."

He started doing a few gigs again with Kris Needs, and began hatching new plans with Potter and France for his next main bid for fame. Eventually he came up with a scheme that had some possibilities for success, but was almost certain to put him even further into debt.

"Chris, you know that £100 that I still owe you for that recording session?" Chris nodded, fully aware of that £100. "Well I've thought of a way to get it back, and make a profit," says Otway.

His idea is, that as no one else will release his recording, he should get someone to manufacture records for him. Chris would lend John the money, and when he has sold all the records, Chris would get that money back, plus his original £100, plus a small profit.

Eventually Chris agreed, as long as the word small did not come before the word profit.

The cheapest place Otway could find to make the records was a small company in Bracknell called County Recording Services. And so, tape recording in hand, our threesome headed off to get their records made.

The headquarters of County Recording Services turned out to be two sheds in the back garden of a suburban house. From which the managing director both manufactured records and mended clocks. As his new clients arrived, they found him busy mending a clock in one of the sheds.

"Oh you came to get some records made, that's over in the other building," he says, leading them over to the other shed.

Otway is fascinated by the place. Being a big fan of both cottage industry and Heath Robinson contraptions, he was delighted to discover perfect examples of them here in suburban Berkshire.

"When cutting the master, I control the speed of the turntable by resting my foot carefully on this flywheel," explained the managing director. Leading them over to the pressing plant he said, "This whole unit is cooled by a well outside the building. We only press five hundred records at a time, because if we press more the well boils over."

The machine Otway found the most fascinating in the whole manufacturing chain however, was the one that removed the excess plastic from the edges of the records after they had been pressed. This remarkable object was at one time an old record player. Instead of a stylus attached to the arm, a large electric soldering iron has been bolted on.

"What we do," the managing director explained to his new clients, "is place the record with all the rough plastic on the outside onto the turntable, spin it round, and lower the soldering iron down by the notch that says seven inches. Of course, if you were making an LP you would use the notch that said 12 inches."

"What do we do about labels then?" John asked. "Ah well, you can get them printed properly, which is quite expensive, or you can use the special labels I've made up with 'County Recording Services' written on them. In fact, why not use these ones here, where I've just used the initials C.R.S. 'cause it reminded me of a big record company."

The deal for five hundred records was concluded. They would take three weeks, during which Otway had promised Chris he would pre-sell the record to all the shops in the area.

John was several years before his time. There had been no independent labels up to then, and going around the shops proved fruitless.

"County Recording Services, never heard of them," the woman behind the counter in the Record Centre in Aylesbury said. "You'll have to ask the manager about this."

"No, I don't think it's the sort of thing we'd be interested in," he said to Otway after John had waited half an hour for him to come back from lunch. "Mind you, if it gets in the Top 40 we'd probably take a few."

As head of his own record company, he hadn't done very well. At the time of the board meeting in The Derby Arms a couple of days before the record was to be released (i.e. the day they were to pick up the five hundred copies), John had not much good news for the head of finance, Chris France.

"Well, seeing as it's my first record, my mum's buying one," he said trying to sound optimistic. "In fact, I've done quite well with my family. It'll be OK when we get the records though. We'll wander round the pub and Friars, and we'll get rid of them like hot cakes."

When they got the records, John's ability as a business man became instantly apparent. He hadn't got any. His first priority with the single was to present signed copies to all the young ladies he either fancied, or thought he could impress.

A copy was immediately put on The Derby Arms juke-box, and Otway would feed money into the machine all night playing it. The result of this constant play meant that everyone in the pub was sick of the sound of it after a week, and the last thing any of them wanted was a copy of "That damn record!"

About the only thing Otway was good at was giving the record away. "If anybody wanted a copy of his record," says Chris, "He would be so delighted, he couldn't wait to give them one. He totally forgot the idea was to sell them. He'd just say things like, 'I can't charge them for one, they're friends', and things like 'If I'd have asked them to pay for it they might not have wanted it anymore'. I got five of my friends to pay full price for them, which is more than you can say for Otway."

Two days after they had the records, Dave Stopps played it at Friars Club between the bands. Dave gave a spiel about the first record by a local artist, and John stood on a table holding up copies of it. Compared to other sales pitches this worked quite well. They actually sold 10 copies that night.

At this time, John and Sue Reece split up. It was a sad time. As he was becoming a recording artiste, he felt he had outgrown the home-town girl who had looked after him through his hard times and helped him with his tent when he was homeless. Sue and her parents felt that someone a little more stable, who was looking for a career, would be a better bet, and John and Sue went their separate ways.

For months after, John would get friends to drive him over to Monks Risborough and get them to take him round the places he remembered so romantically. He also poured out songs and sent them to her, and for the first time in his life, he felt true heartache.

The emotional periods of Otway's life were always his most prolific, and this was one of them. He wrote many songs for his childhood sweetheart, as he attempted to come to terms with his failure in combining his relationship with his career.

Some of these songs, like 'Bluey Green' and 'Place Farm Way' had a pleasant naïve quality to them, and would be recorded later. Others like 'Long Lonely Time', written whilst he was at his soppiest, were just wet. They started with lines like 'Last night I wept you were not there, beside me in my bed.' "I sometimes wondered what Sue thought of that song after I sent it to her," John says now.

This was a period of partings, some temporary, others not so. Potter had passed an 'A'-level and got a place at a teacher training college.

"It's better than working," he said as he packed his bags for Exeter. "Don't worry, the moment it hits the charts I'll be back."

Otway helped him to the bus station with his bags. He felt, with both Potter and his girlfriend gone, a little lonely.

One night at about 11.30 pm, just after John had gone to bed, his mum came to his room to tell him there was a girl on the phone who wanted to speak to him urgently. As he picked up the phone he could hear his record playing. No one spoke until it was over, then John Peel's voice told Otway that he had been listening to a new song by John Otway called 'Gypsy'.

What surprised John was not the information, he knew all that, but that John Peel was giving it to him over the phone. All was revealed when Jacky, one of the girls to whom John had presented a signed copy of his record, came on the phone and said ecstatically: "You're on the radio, you're on Radio One!" Otway then woke the rest of the household with the good news.

This one radio play of 'Misty Mountain'/'Gypsy' helped the passionate side of Otway's life, because Jacky was impressed by it. It did not increase sales of the single though, even with an 'As heard on Radio One' sign attached to the copy of the record above the saloon bar of The Derby Arms.

Otway had decided to leave Willy's name off that first record. The reasons for this were two-fold: first John was still unhappy about the Barrett Car episode, and second, he wanted to make sure Willy did not try and claim the lion's share of the profit from the record.

Willy, meanwhile, had been spending less and less time in Aylesbury. Having regained a little credibility after getting rid of Otway, he had found a manager in London, who was starting to get him higher profile gigs.

Ian King, his new manager, ran BIT, a helpline and information service from the Westbourne Park area of London. This was a time of free concerts and benefit gigs. The connection between BIT and the music scene in London at the time was strong, and an environment that Willy found both invigorating and exciting.

Otway sent Willy some copies of the record. "I felt I had to," John says. "I mean, he had played on it and produced it. Even though we'd fallen out, I thought it was only fair to send him a few copies. It wasn't as if I didn't have any left."

A few days after he had received the singles, Willy called up John and told him that he had important news, and that they had to meet.

Otway was concerned. Willy wanted something. Was it a share of the profit from the record? Our recording star was worried. So worried in fact, that he refused to meet Willy on his own.

"Look it doesn't matter who the hell is there," said Barrett impatiently, "I just need to see you."

With Potter gone and no henchman by his side, Otway pulled in Paul Kendall to help him in the meeting. Paul Kendall had been at Queens Park with Otway. He had passed his 11-plus a year early, and was now at Oxford University. Otway and Kendall had re-met at the pub, and John figured that he must be a pretty clever bloke to have achieved all this.

John reckoned that Paul would be able to see through whatever devious plan Willy had in mind. Chris France was also summoned to the meeting to make sure that John did not get ripped off financially.

"Just don't let me get talked into working with him again," Otway insisted to them before that meeting. "I don't care if he has got blonde hair. I know I'm a little impressionable, that's why you're here, so I don't get sucked into anything and end up living in a tent."

CHAPTER
9

Having received the copies of 'Misty Mountain'/'Gypsy', Willy had played the record to Ian King, who quite liked it. As it featured Willy's playing, Ian passed copies on to whatever influential people he knew. Among these were John Peel and Pete Townshend.

Pete Townshend called Ian King back and said he liked the record. Would the artists be interested in him producing a proper version of the 'Misty Mountain' song? It was the sort of offer that no manager turns down or thinks twice about. Without checking with Willy, he said, "Of course the artists would be more than delighted," and went to tell Willy the great news.

This news was a mixed blessing for Willy. When he had dropped John off at The Derby, he really thought he had seen the last of him. The fact that he knew Otway wanted no more to do with him was a positive advantage. Willy was pleased with the way things were going in London too. Ian King, along with a concert promoter Errol D'Silva, had sorted him out with a van and a sound system.

"But Otway's a loony," Willy tried explaining to Ian King. "You don't realise, any attempt to work with him either ends up a disaster or losing a lot of money, or both".

Ian King pointed out to Willy that the sort of opportunity that was being offered was a once in a lifetime break, and, as he had already put his neck on the line, Willy ought to patch it up with John. They should at least give it a go.

And so it was that Willy in his new van headed back to Aylesbury for the meeting with John and his two 'advisors'.

"I don't give two hoots about my name not being on the record," Willy said. "And yes, you can keep all the profit from the records. Pete Townshend has offered to produce the record for us. If we take the offer up we will have no difficulty getting a proper recording contract, and the last thing he produced – 'Something In The Air', by Thunderclap Newman – was a number one hit record. John, surely you can see that what we are talking about here is not some little local thing, it's a real opportunity, with a chance of real success."

Otway asked Willy to leave the room while he discussed this offer with his advisors. "I can see what Willy is up to here," John told Paul and Chris. "Basically he is miffed that he didn't think of making a record first, and he wants to get on the bandwagon now that I'm a recording artist. This Pete Townshend thing is just a smoke screen. If I take him up on the offer I'll be back in a tent in no time, don't you agree?"

Chris France started going pale. He most certainly did not agree. A chance was here to make a real profit and Otway was about to blow it. Paul Kendall started wondering if all his years of education had taught him enough to use the English language in a manner that would make Otway see sense and reason.

"But you're taking his side," Otway grumbled as they tried to get through to him. Eventually Paul Kendall's study and learning in the English language paid off: "Stop being such a bloody stupid wally!" he said, getting up to leave. "You asked me to come here to give you some advice, and I'm giving you it. For Christ's sake at least go and meet Pete Townshend."

Otway called Willy back into the room and told him that although he did not believe the Townshend story, Paul and Chris, against his better judgement, had persuaded him to follow it up.

It was arranged for John, Willy and Ian King to go round to Pete Townshend's house to talk about the forthcoming production. They had been asked to take a guitar and fiddle, so they could play 'Misty Mountain' to their new producer. All the way from Aylesbury to Twickenham, Otway kept saying to Willy that he knew there was no Pete Townshend. Paul and Chris might be taken in by the story, but the joke would be on those two, not himself, when the legendary guitarist failed to appear.

Eventually they arrived at Twickenham and drew up outside a large house by the River Thames, and Pete opened the door to his new artistes.

"I really didn't believe that this was going to happen," says John, "So I hadn't prepared myself for it at all. Suddenly there was this guy, and it really was Pete Townshend. I was speechless most of the time. When he asked us if we could play the song through to him, I suddenly realised that I was going to have to play my guitar in front of one of the world's most famous guitarists."

It probably was not the most confident performance of the song the duo had ever performed, but Pete seemed happy enough. He said he would organise a studio and a drummer and he would play bass on the track himself.

On the way home from that meeting, John thought it might be wise to bury the hatchet with Willy. And so, after splitting up twice, they decided to get together for a third time.

Potter heard the news while at Exeter. He decided that now Pete Townshend was involved in his friend's career, there was no point in even waiting for a hit. He packed his bags, said goodbye to Exeter College, and came back to Aylesbury ready and waiting to join in the fun and glamour of stardom. All thoughts of selling a record went totally out of the window and Chris was quite happy to wait a little longer to get the £300 John now owed him.

Olympic Studios in Barnes was a completely different place to Pro-Musica in Maidenhead. It was huge. Studio One is an old converted cinema, large enough to take a complete symphony orchestra, while Pro-Musica was a converted basement of a music shop, large enough to take a four piece band (if the singer sang in the hall).

Methods of recording were also considerably different. In Pro-Musica you played the track once, listened back to it, and then ran around the studio yelling "It's a hit, it's a hit."

At Olympic things took a little longer. And there was no yelling – especially in front of Pete Townshend. (Actually John did yell a little, but that was in the toilets when he thought no one could hear.)

Pete Townshend had got Speedy Keen to play drums on the track. Speedy was Thunderclap Newman's drummer, who had written the number one song 'Something In The Air', a fact which Otway believed was an omen for the forthcoming record.

Pete and Speedy spent a couple of hours putting down a rhythm track for the song, before it was John's turn to play his guitar part. It did not take too long to work out that Pete's playing sounded better than John's, so Pete played guitar as well as bass. Willy's fiddle playing sounded great and did not take too long at all.

At around 2 am on October 15, 1972, Otway went into that great old cinema auditorium to sing his vocals.

Whenever he is either nervous or showing off, Otway employs a wild uncoordinated style of performance. On this occasion, he was nervous and showing off at the same time, and because of the time in the morning, Otway's first vocal attempt had everyone in the control room rolling around in hysterics.

"What was so odd," says Otway, "is that it seemed to have the same effect on them that playing at Green Park had on the orchestra."

In fact, it wasn't odd at all. At Green Park you had serious musicians who were good at what they did, watching some nutter who wasn't. At Olympic studios you had the same thing.

Pete Townshend managed, over the next couple of hours, to capture the wildness and humour of John's performance and lose its excesses. In the end, everyone was very happy, and as John walked back into the control room, some chap came up to him and said, "That was very good mate."

Otway by now was in no mood for modesty, and replied, "Yeah I know, it was wasn't it?" A few seconds later, Willy and Ian King managed to get John to one side and ask him what Mick Jagger had said to him.

They spent two long days at Olympic Studios. The finished result was the first professional recording John had done.

"It's pretty good," they agreed, as they left Olympic after it had been mixed. And so Pete Townshend and Ian King went off to find a record company to take it.

One need not state the effect this had on Otway: it would be a "hit before Christmas".

"I really have made it," he thought to himself. "All those years of hardship and determination have paid off. I am now where I want to be, in the same studios and in league with the greatest stars in the world."

CHAPTER 10

While John awaited his first record deal, he continued working at British Rail as a booking clerk. As they were now proper recording artistes, John and Willy started doing a few gigs together again. Optimism seemed to do the world of good for them both and they were each making the necessary effort to get on well, and to put together a show that successfully combined Willy's playing talent with Otway's extravagant theatrical style. If John could not win the audience with the wild bit, Willy could do it with his bluegrass fiddle playing.

This combination worked well at times: Willy seemed to be the one person who had any degree of control over Otway on stage. If Willy felt that what Otway was doing was wrong, he would do things like get a broom and sweep him off stage, or simply slap him around the head.

On one occasion, playing late night at Kings Cross Cinema, the duo were introduced by the MC.

"A big hand please for John Otway and Willy Barrett." After they had played their set, he announced: "Ladies and gentlemen, Willy Barrett and John Otway." At the end of the encore he joined in the applause, saying "That was great. Thank you Willy Barrett and his mate."

Often people would walk up to Willy and say, "Hey, you were really good, what are you doing working with the nutter?"

But there were also some good shows where they both worked well together and occasionally the embryo of a successful stage act could be seen.

As the year wore on, it became obvious that the record deal that had been such a certainty was not going to happen quite as quickly as hoped. Pete Townshend thought that the big studio sound of the recording was probably a little too big for what was originally a pretty folky sort of song. But he was still interested in helping if he could.

John and Willy had discovered they could make good demos by wiring together bits of the sound system (that Willy had got from BIT) to some old tape recorders.

One week, when John's parents were away, number six, Ash Grove became a recording studio. Paul Kendall had bought himself a bass guitar and so he was brought in to play bass. Paul Burt, an old schoolfriend that several people (including John and Willy) had used as a roadie on shows, was brought in as engineer. Potter and France were brought in as spectators, and the whole lot moved in for the week.

"It was just as well my folks were away," John says. "The whole place was worse than the zip episode. Paul Burt had turned my bedroom into a studio control room: there was a whole P.A. system, three Grundig tape recorders, and masses of wire running down to the studio we'd built in the living room and kitchen. As well as a residential area, the dining room was full of amplifiers for the bass and things. And there were speakers around everywhere for Paul to talk to us from upstairs while we were recording."

It was the end of a year that had had its share of heartbreaks and trauma, and therefore John had written quite a lot of songs By the end of that hard week's work in 'Ash Grove Studios', they had about nine or 10 reasonable sounding songs recorded.

Early in the new year of 1973, John and Willy travelled up to Twickenham to play them to Pete Townshend. He was quite impressed, and suggested that they record the most promising of the songs in the eight-track studio he had built in his house.

They were enjoyable times for the duo. Willy would pick up John from the railway station where he was working and they would travel up to Pete's place to record for the rest of the day. Eventually they picked a track that they thought sounded the most like a single and took it to Track records, The Who's record company, who agreed to release it.

The single was based on an instrumental Willy used to play called 'Hair On The Frets'. John wrote some lyrics about his sad romance with Sue Reece, and called it 'Lonely Man'. Eventually everyone agreed that the Otway lyrics could stay if he made the chorus a little less soppy, and the song became 'Murder Man'.

A release date was set for the day before Good Friday, and for the second time in his life, John decided now he could truly afford to go professional.

The next few weeks were fun. Both the *Bucks Herald* and the *Bucks Advertiser* wanted to do pieces on the duo's new record. Track records called to say that they had managed to get the record released in the USA, and John managed to get his own back on The Record Centre in Aylesbury. "I want to order ten copies of my new record, it's on Track Records. The Who are on that label, have you heard of them?" he enquired sarcastically. "That's shown them!" he thought as he handed over a fiver to the woman behind the counter.

The day arrived and the record, along with about two hundred other singles that week, was released. Steve Peacock, who remembered John from Hobble On The Cobbles, reviewed it in *Sounds* and called it, "A really nice single... one of the most delightful records of the week," while John Peel played it and said, "It's a strange and lovely record and I hope it sells millions and that you like it. I think you will."

In the end, the record shop that sold by far and away the most copies of the record was The Record Centre in Aylesbury.

Otway's career took a couple of steps backwards: Pete Townshend had now started work on the new Who album which was to become 'Quadrophenia', and had to cut down on his other commitments including Otway and Barrett; and distractions in the form of romance had again entered into the life of our star. John had started going out with Patricia Trewavas – a relationship doomed to failure, as Patricia was both intelligent and sensible.

The next big event in the Aylesbury Calendar was Rabens Rock, a free pop festival organised by Dave Stopps in a field next to the sewage works. Quite high on that bill was to be the Pete Townshend-produced duo, Otway and Barrett. Two thousand turned up to that event, which was the largest audience John had played to since Hobble On The Cobbles.

The fond memories of reading the *Sounds* review came flooding back into John's mind, and, while Willy attempted to hold the show together musically, Otway put the same 'energy' into this show as he did in the Market Square two years before. Their own reaction to this performance shows an ideological split which was threatening this volatile duo.

"That was the turning point for us," Willy said later, "I was so appalled by his performance. It was the height of the period when people were coming up to me and asking, 'Why was I working with an idiot like that?' I had no answer to give them."

The *Bucks Advertiser* praised Willy's expertise but claimed that John was "out of his depth". but Otway said: "I was really pleased with it. I thought it was just like the old days, you know with the wild Otway."

John was not the only one to enjoy his performance that day though. A young 16-year-old girl called Pauline Thompson had been watching his antics and fallen for him. It has always been rare for Otway to be greeted backstage by attractive young ladies, and John, because he was never loved by them when younger, had this complicated problem of falling in love with anyone who fell in love with him.

For a while, John had to split his time between his career, Patricia Trewavas, and Pauline Thompson. This situation could not last, and, because of lack of forethought on Otway's behalf, came to an abrupt end after his next major career move. This move managed to split up both Otway and Barrett and John and Patricia, as well as getting him so deep into debt that it would take a hit record some three years later to get out of.

"That was the final straw for me. It was such a stupid idea that it's not worth talking about," said Willy.

The next move came because of the lack of instant fame from the single. John was baffled. "What does it take to achieve success?" he thought, and went into a short period of soul-searching and self analysis.

For most people, looking inward is a therapeutic device, which helps them see where they have gone awry in the past, and apply those lessons to make their lives richer and more rewarding in the future. For people like Otway, looking inward is a highly dangerous process, and the result of such meditation can usually be summed up in one word: expensive.

"I think I should make a film," he announced one night in The Derby Arms. "My talent is basically visual, and my art comes down to the charismatic quality of my live show." "You mean that a lot of people laugh when you throw yourself around the stage?" Chris asked.

"Yes," John replied. "Look, if I can achieve what I've just achieved by making a record, think of what can be achieved and how much can be gained by making a film."

Sadly no one was there to point out that by making a record he had achieved a debt of £300. And that by making a film, he could gain a debt considerably larger. Otway probably would not have listened anyway. He had his heart set on the film, and in these situations he is stubborn.

He went in search of a film director, and was introduced to Geoff Husson. "Yes," said Geoff, "I'll do it, but it will be costly to do it properly. I could do a cheaper film for you, but you wouldn't be able to use it for broadcast on television. It would still look good though, and show what you can do."

Otway was adamant. He needed to be on TV if he was to be a household name. Whatever film he made, it had to be "made for the airwaves."

His attitude towards money was simple. He was destined to be a star, and when he was, he would have lots and lots of it. Why care if he got into debt now, sooner or later he would be able to pay off anything he owed. The people who lent him money would eventually be pleased they had, because he would be generous to those who had helped him on this rocky road to fame.

He also knew that there was no way that he could raise the whole amount necessary to make this epic in one go. What he would do was raise the finance stage-by-stage as it was required. Chris France was the obvious first move. It was suggested that the debt should be rounded up to £500, "because that's an easy figure to remember." This extra £200 would pay for the initial film, the lights and the hire of the hall.

Geoff Husson was a professional film director, and as such had never worked with someone like John before. John played the two Pete Townshend productions he wished to mime to, and Geoff went away to make up a shooting script. Geoff had worked on many film projects before and could be forgiven for thinking that what his star wanted was something that made him look as good as possible. What John had failed to get across to his new director, was that he wanted a film that made him look as silly as possible.

To give the film some atmosphere it had been decided to add a small live audience, which could be easily found in The Derby Arms. But there was a problem. Both Patricia and Pauline were more than willing to come and help John out. John felt, quite accurately, that Pauline would be the most impressed watching him work for the first time in front of the cameras, and so invited her along.

"I know this is hard to understand," John said to Patricia, "but I'm going to be so nervous on the day, and you know how I worry about you, it would make it easier for me if I could just concentrate on what I was doing. You will get to see the finished thing though."

John arrived early for his first and only day on set: he was after all both producer and star in his own epic. The film was to be shot on the stage of the Borough Assembly Hall, the scene of some of Otway's early triumphs at the Friars club. The two numbers to be filmed were 'Misty Mountain' and 'If I Did'. Most of the day went something like this:

"So which way do I do the somersault with the guitar?" Otway asked the director. "Er... somersault with guitar, Er... yes... well you can do that if you like but as we are going to be doing a close up of your face, I think the camera might not catch it all," he replied.

"Er... John? I'm not quite sure what you are doing wiggling the guitar between your knees like that, but we are still doing a close up of your face."

"John, as this is a close up of your face, it would probably look a little better if you moved your lips in time to the words on the recording."

"John, if you were going to do something like that, it might have been helpful if you had been doing it when the camera was on you. As we are shooting Willy's fiddle solo, it is just a little distracting." And so the day went on.

Three days later John went back to Geoff Husson and asked, "What happens next?"

"The processing, editing, neg cutting, dubbing and printing of the finished film." he was told. "Is that expensive?" "It's about £600."

"Oh," said John, "I thought we'd done the expensive bit, with all the cameras and lights and things like that. I don't know if Chris France has got another £600."

For once John was quite astute. Chris certainly did not have another £600. "And if you manage to borrow that much," Chris asked, "When do I get the £500 back?"

In the end there was nothing for it. John had to ask his parents. Mr and Mrs Otway had watched their one and only son go from disaster to disaster in search of a career he was not much good at, and did not want to see him waste away his life on false dreams. If they were to lend him the money, would he do a deal with them? If the film did not work out and bring him great riches, would he once and for all get a proper job and earn a sensible living?

The thinking behind this is not too difficult to grasp. Although £600 was a lot of money, it seemed a small amount to fork out if John was indeed going to settle down afterwards and do something reasonable with his life. It was a nice try, and had it worked, would have been money well spent.

Now Otway was able to finish the film, and on completion one of the first people he proudly showed it to was Patricia Trewavas.

"John, that's Pauline Thompson in the front row of the audience!" she exploded. "You promised me you had never seen her since I caught you kissing her at Rabens Rock."

And so she walked out on him. Eventually, she would have the good sense to go out with, and marry, Paul Kendall.

John had hired a 16mm projector to take the film around and show to people. "I don't know if he did much of that," says Potter. "I went round his house one day and he came rushing out screaming 'I'm on telly, I'm on telly.' He had worked out how to project the film onto his TV screen at home, which looked pretty good if he closed the curtains. We spent the whole day in his living room watching him."

Otway had actually booked several appointments with record companies to show his film and they duly got a visit from John, his film, and his projection equipment. He was, as with his own indie record label, well before his time. Record companies had not yet got into the concept of video artists.

"The problem was," John says, "That it took me about half an hour to set the projector up in an office. And when I'd done that, most of the offices were so small that the largest picture I could get on the screen was about 10 inches by eight. At that size you couldn't focus it properly. I often asked them if they had a telly I could project it on to, but they always seemed to be saying, 'Can't you just play a tape?' which meant that there was no point in spending all this money on a film."

Willy was not happy either. Ian King and Erroll D'silva were working hard on his behalf trying to get Barrett a deal on his own. It did not help that whenever they rang up companies, it seemed that John and the film had been there first.

John did, however, manage to get the film shown between the bands at Friars one night. It also got shown to the Girl Guides when John's mum, who had become a Girl Guide captain, borrowed the film to accompany a film about campfire cooking. Apart from these showings, the film has remained in obscurity ever since.

Sadly, John knew that having failed so badly, he would now have to get another job and fulfil his part of the bargain with his parents. His belief in his destiny, though, was still unshaken, and he took this last disaster as one of the downs that Mrs Clerk had told him he would have before his eventual success.

John applied for, and got, a job at CBS records, packing LPs into boxes. He had noticed a while ago in the local paper a piece on Steve Ellis from the group Love Affair, who was being taken around the factory and shown how his records were made. Otway thought that when he was a star, his factory tour would make a much better piece in the paper if he had already worked there beforehand.

"I could then be quoted saying 'I know how hard these people work to make sure I have hits' and things like that," Otway says.

John was very conscious of what he might have to say to the media once his career had taken off. And his bizarre thought processes came up with the strangest things.

"Chris do you think you could manage to book me to play at some Women's Institutes?" John asked one night.

"What on earth for?" Chris replied, waiting for the punchline of the joke. "I was thinking. When I do interviews later on, it would be far more fun to say things like, 'Oh yes, I used to do that when I was playing the WIs,' than to say I was doing it in rock clubs," John replied.

And he was serious. Chris had a hard time getting these bookings for Otway, and did not see any reduction in the debt. But Chris was a good friend, and John can now proudly say. "When I played Princess Risborough Wife and Home Club," or, "One night after the Beetle Drive at Burndine Women's Institute..."

CHAPTER 12

After a couple of months, John was not only aware of how hard people worked at the CBS factory to make hits, he was also sick of working hard to make hits for other people. He decided he would have to find another job. Using the formula he had used in deciding on this last employment, he wondered what would sound good in interviews later on. The first idea he came up with was a lavatory attendant in the toilets in the new town centre.

"Yeah, that would have been a corker," he says. "I could have said things like, 'I had a very convenient job' or 'It was the one place I worked where people came in and did the jobs!' and horrid things like that. It would have been really funny. But in the end I didn't think it was really fair on my parents. I had put them through quite a lot, and I don't think it would have been very nice for them to admit to their friends that their only son was a toilet cleaner."

He ended up getting the one job he ever says he quite enjoyed, which must have some truth in it, as this one lasted over two years. He became a dustman.

"I thought that was a pretty good compromise, and it was good fun. You started early in the morning, and finished early in the afternoon. I was on country rounds most of the time around the little villages surrounding Aylesbury – Buckinghamshire is a beautiful county and I got to see a lot of it in a way that few people do. I could also sing at work which was nice. The other blokes on the round used to think it was a bit strange, me singing all the time, but that job had a tendency to attract eccentric people anyway."

Pauline had moved to Evesham as her father had found a new job there and Otway started spending most weekends in Worcestershire. It is easy to follow the courtship of John and Pauline, as Otway kept a diary at this time.

"We used to ask John if we could borrow his diary to see what gigs he had coming up, and then count the amount of hearts that had appeared since the last time we'd looked. That boy had such a romantic view of sex," says Potter. "Sometimes he would get moody and worried for a few days, so we'd check his diary for her last period, and then start teasing him about babies."

"I must say me and Pauline weren't very sensible," admits John. "I don't think a month went by without having to worry about little Otways."

This concern did bring out the creative side of our artist though, and sometimes the worry brought out an almost broody side of his character which is wonderfully depicted in the thankfully unreleased 'Dreaming Babies':

> *They say you're late again*
> *I can tell you how happy I am*
> *And though your friends say what a fool you've been*
> *Don't worry I will hold your hand*
> *'Cause I've been Dreaming Babies*
> *Sha la la*
> *They'll smile when they see*
> *What Beautiful Parents we are*
> *She gave me her permission*
> *She didn't know what she'd given*
> *A glowing flame*
> *That would burn the hearts of a million*

One song that was later released gives us some idea of the more practical and frantic side of this problem, a song called 'Baby's In The Club':

> *I've been worried all night*
> *I had to leave on the light*
> *So the room didn't spin*
> *I'd been drinking hard*
> *Often I wondered what I'd do if this happened*
> *And I don't know now that it has*
> *Baby's in the club.*

Otway met up with Kris Needs again in the spring of 1984, and discovered that his old bongo player was now working as a journalist for the local paper the *Bucks Advertiser*. Never one to miss an opportunity for media exposure, Otway suggested that the two of them get back together to do some gigs.

The problem was that there were not many places to play, which seemed a bit of a waste to Otway, who had now found an easy way to get local newspaper exposure. John, as ever, employed his technique of doing something expensive when faced with a problem of this type.

He had long wanted to do a concert in the town, which he could both headline and fill. John knew that there were no more than 20 people in Aylesbury that would be willing to pay to see him, and not many more that would come even if they didn't have to pay. But, as he had learnt in the past, no problem is too big if you can borrow enough money to solve it.

His solution was The John Otway Free Concert. Otway hired Bedgrove Pavilion in Aylesbury, and persuaded a couple of local bands, who could fill the place, to come and play.

Otway took this event very seriously. He hired a massive PA and a huge lighting rig, that took up a large area of the hall. He had hundreds of posters and handouts printed, and booked a substantial amount of advertising in the local press.

Willy meanwhile had been doing very well. He had secured himself a recording deal with Transatlantic Records and, as he had not made a film or anything like that, he did not have to work as a dustman to pay off debts. John asked Willy if he would play at his free concert, and Willy, very wary of any Otway scheme, said no. However, were Otway to book studio time, he would be prepared to record some backing tapes so John could sing along to his playing. "Basically I'll do anything as long as I don't have to get on stage with him," said Willy.

A few years before all this, John had met an old lady who claimed she was psychic. She had told him that he should wear earrings, as it would be very lucky for him. During this period of his life, John needed all the luck he could get, so Paul Burt, the roadie, was summoned to Ash Grove with his red hot darning needle, his ice cubes and his wine cork to perform the necessary operation.

The concert went very well. The support bands did draw the crowds as expected, but Otway's performance was patchy, as neither John or Kris Needs could keep in time with the backing tapes which had taken Willy a week to record. By the end of the night though, there were enough funny bits to amuse the audience and, as it was a free concert, everyone was in a pretty good mood.

A recording of this concert still exists. Unfortunately, the microphone was placed next to Paul Burt, the earpiercer, who can be heard much louder than Otway saying things like, "Christ this is awful!" and "How can we get him off?"

John was rewarded for all his effort. Kris Needs, under another name, had written a piece for the front page of the *Bucks Advertiser* which started, "Dustman by day, pop star by night..." and went on to say how good the bongo playing was. It was Otway's first front page. Being a dustman had its advantages – the following week while John was doing the rounds, he managed to collect 75 copies of that front page.

This brief flurry of excitement and local fame soon died however, and the summer slipped by quietly, if not lazily, judging by the number of hearts in Otway's diary. Under the surface, nevertheless, things were bubbling which were soon to have an effect on Otway's career and lifestyle.

CHAPTER 13

In Aylesbury Market Square there is a hotel called The Bell. Tamburlain, a local folk group, had started a folk night and played there every Thursday. They were a popular group and the saloon bar was filled to capacity each time they played.

John first appeared there on September 5, 1974, and because of both his performance and local notoriety went down with a success that guaranteed further appearances.

After six weeks of Tamburlain, the manager of The Bell was looking for someone else to take over the folk night, and Otway was both able and willing to run it.

Folk night under Otway's management soon became Rock night, although it retained the name folk. The Bell paid £20 for the entertainment each week – John booked the acts for £15 and kept a fiver for running it. When he was broke, he booked himself and kept all the money.

Having a regular venue to play was a luxury for Otway which he made the most of. One night, after finding a pile of Dexion angle iron in his dad's shed, he built a long metal stage with a platform that reached halfway into the bar.

"It was only a couple of feet wide, and four feet off the ground," remembers Potter. "I went round to his house on the afternoon John had built it and was trying it out in the garden. He would stand at one end and somersault with the guitar. He fell off the first couple of times he tried it, but had got it right by the time he got to re-erect it at The Bell."

John became attractive to several of the young ladies who used to frequent the folk night. "He seems so useless and incapable," one of them said, "that you just want to take him home and look after him." The problem was that when they took him home, they did more than just look after him. Because

John would literally fall for anyone that liked him, he never got used to the fact that he only needed one person to look after him at a time.

As these problems increased in severity, Otway felt he needed to escape and asked Pete Frame if he could stay at his home a few miles out of Aylesbury, and a few miles out of trouble.

Pete Frame was the editor of a music paper called *Zigzag*, which was a successful monthly music magazine concentrating on West Coast American rock bands. What these groups had in common with Otway's style of music is uncertain, but he had watched the career of our hero with growing interest for a few years. He had just got himself a job at Charisma Records, and felt that he might be able to help Otway's career. He suggested that maybe he should manage the young star and help him achieve his aims. Pete lived in a beautiful Tudor thatched cottage. When Otway moved in Pete educated him with his collection of three thousand LPs, and for the first few days things seemed to work out OK.

Under Otway's supervision, Pete's two Alsatian dogs would escape the cottage at least three times a day, Pete's kitchen would look like a bomb site within seconds of Otway entering the room, and it is amazing how a collection of three thousand records can all end up in the wrong covers in one evening if John is given the opportunity of playing DJ.

The house-sharing arrangement came to an end after Pete spotted John's size 11 foot hanging from the top of his cupboard. "That staircase has been there for four hundred years and it has never broken," he quite accurately pointed out. And so John had to move back to Aylesbury and face the women.

The difficulties of continuing a romance between Aylesbury and Evesham, as well as the new female fans, had been too much of a strain on Pauline, who now had a more stable relationship in her home town, and the hearts in Otway's diary cease from this point.

In order to raise his profile in The Bell, Otway had an idea. To an outsider, it was simply to run a magazine for the folk night. But to anyone who had an insight into the way his mind worked, it was in fact a piece of propaganda to advertise himself. Otway had paid Paul Kendall to write his biography in six parts, and yes, the magazine ran for only six editions. Publication stopped abruptly after the final chapter of the Otway Story. Compared to the two pages per issue containing the Otway Story, Willy did not fare quite so well. He had half a page in one issue penned by John himself.

"Willy's big break," it read, "happened when John Otway took him into a studio and made him into a recording artist." It continued in a similar vein. As a magazine it was quite interesting and created considerable anguish, chaos and heartache among the regulars at The Bell during its short period of publication.

Chris France thought it would be highly entertaining to run a gossip column on the back page, and Otway didn't really care as long as a chapter of his story went in each issue. Chris' gossip page was called *The Bellcher*, and as organiser of the page, Chris discovered a talent in himself that he had hitherto been unaware of. He found that as the anonymous writer, by linking names fictitiously or not, happy stable relationships could be turned into disastrous partnerships of seething hatred. He would get together a small group at Ash Grove, and at the head of the table in control of the typewriter, would gather and manipulate any piece of gossip gleaned from the assembled company.

He was a natural. For some reason, everyone seemed quite happy to give him information about others, but felt it was completely unfair when the person they loved dearly swiped them across the face because of something they had read in *The Bellcher*. Because of Chris' influence, the magazine became a scurrilous little paper loved by all but those people featured within its pages.

One snippet in *The Bellcher* read, "The Magenta lipstick, we name the guilty men." The Magenta lipstick referred to a girl called Kim Taylor, one of the most extraordinary looking girls to ever grace The Bell Folk Night. She had intensely violent dyed red hair, and wore clothes and make up that were as shocking and unbelievable as her crowning glory. After this small mention she adopted the name Magenta and it has stuck ever since.

John liked Magenta – she was, and looked, outrageous. "The first time I saw her I thought 'Wow, I ought to go out with her. She really is the sort of person I should be seen with'."

But his efforts at wooing her backfired badly. He and Potter worked out a plan. Jeff would go to The Bell that night and say to Magenta, "Please thank John for the flowers, he gave me £20 to send you some by Interflora, but I put the money on a horse which came in last. As long as you tell him you got them, he'll be happy and none the wiser."

Thus John was able to convince this girl that he'd spent a fortune on flowers for her, without having to fork out a penny. Unfortunately she was far more impressed with Potter's more sensible investment of the fictitious £20 than she was with

Otway's, and she and Potter went out with each other steadily for the next few years.

Chris had watched the success of The Bell Folk Night with interest. It was a time when Pub Rock was becoming fashionable, and Chris instinctively knew that there was money to be made. He found a hotel in Leighton Buzzard, eight miles outside Aylesbury, called The Hunt Hotel, and started promoting shows. Within a couple of months, Chris was running not only the Hunt, but another five venues locally, three within the town of Aylesbury.

Chris managed to book blossoming London acts like XTC and The Jam for as little as £30, although local bands (Otway included) could be persuaded to play for as little as £10. Because it was cheaper for Chris, more and more local bands managed to get more and more local gigs, and for a while we had a burgeoning little music scene in the town.

Pete Frame picked up on what was happening in Aylesbury, and decided to start a local music paper to help his protégé. He had seen the success that small fanzines in New York had in making cult heroes out of local acts. Pete felt, with all these things happening in the town, it would be possible to portray Aylesbury as England's answer to the Big Apple upon the pages of a magazine.

The paper was called *The Roxette*. The front page of each issue featured a local act, and its pages were filled with all the gossip and music news from the hippest town in the land.

Some, though not all, of the writing and creative staff of The Bell Magazine joined *The Roxette*. Magenta DeVine was given the gossip column. She looked much trendier than Chris France and her writing style was considerably less vicious. Chris was given the less destructive job of selling advertising.

Otway loved the idea. As it was explained to him, he felt the same rush of enthusiasm as he did when Miss Williams told the class she was going to start the *Alpha Mail*. The first issue even contained an article about the British Library being sent a copy.

It was not only the British Library who received copies. All the music press, record companies, radio stations and the media in general became aware of just what a happening town Aylesbury had become. Because Pete Frame, the editor of the much-respected *Zigzag* magazine, said the place was "like Liverpool in the sixties", then it must be.

The Otway shows were reviewed regularly in *The Roxette* – Magenta kept readers up to date with Otway gossip and no issue of the paper was produced that did not contain a photo of Aylesbury's most famous dustman. It was by far the most publicity John had had so far.

One night at Friars, Otway met and fell in love with a young 16-year-old girl called Lisa Borowic. "I don't know what hit me," he says.

"I could not work that out at all" says Chris, "She was nice enough, but nothing out of the ordinary. She was also quite quiet, which didn't help as Otway was dumbstruck and just kept hovering around her with his mouth open. After extolling her virtues at me for half an hour, he persuaded me to somehow set up a date with her."

Setting up a date with Lisa was easier said than done. Lisa was boarding at an exclusive girls school deep in the Chiltern Hills seven miles out of town. The school and its rules had been designed in a way that made contact between its pupils and boys like Otway extremely difficult. Had it not been for the input of the devious Mr France, contact would have been impossible. As it was, contact was brief, and long enough only to break John's heart.

The girls were allowed one phone call a week at a specified time, and were not allowed calls from boyfriends at all. They were allowed out one Saturday in four, and then only if they were with an adult approved by the school.

Chris France knew Rachael, a daughter of one of the teachers in the school, and asked her out. As her mother was obviously an approved guardian, Chris managed to organise a foursome. "The things I did for Otway," says Chris.

On that Saturday walk on the hills, John managed to hold Lisa's hand, kiss her and become totally infatuated. He also acquired the name Uncle George so he could talk to her once a week, during the allowed phone call. However, the holidays were coming up and she was flying home to her parents in Switzerland.

The last time John saw Lisa, and the only other time they kissed, was in the Terminal Two building at Heathrow Airport. John was wearing his suit, had his hair cut by a real barber, and was sporting brand new 12- carat gold earrings.

"We'd planned this meeting for weeks," says John, "It was very romantic. I was hoping to fly over to Geneva to meet her in a couple of weeks, and we could have spent some time alone together."

For the next few days, John was seen carrying around a huge slab of A4 paper and writing furiously. "New songs?" friends would enquire. "No, I'm writing to Lisa," John would reply. "It's a rather long letter isn't it?" they would say.

And they were right, it was indeed a rather long letter. Forty pages of closely written Otway scrawl, that dwarfed his earlier *Rumplestiltskin* epic poem by a factor of about 10 to one.

Within these almost illegible pages, John poured out his life story, his philosophy, his dreams for the future and an explanation of his burning desire for Lisa, this unassuming quiet girl for whom he felt so much.

What she felt when she received this long tome is unknown. A few days after it had been sent by express airmail, John got a message saying that she had found someone in Switzerland and did not want to see him any more. Otway got the news on arrival back from the travel agents, where he had been arranging his long journey to the Alps.

"John was devastated and went into a decline for weeks," remembers Potter. "I've never known anyone be as upset over someone that they'd met three times and kissed twice."

Otway made an attempt to win her back the only way he knew how, by writing songs and sending them to her.

"I spent ages writing those songs," Otway says. "I was really hurt and desperately wanted her to know how I felt."

Potter remembers John inviting him around to play some songs just after this. "He hadn't written much in ages, and we were all on at him asking him when he was going to write some new material. There had been a burst of stuff after the Sue Reece and Pete Townshend time, and nothing at all after it. I didn't even know he'd been writing. Suddenly, he had this whole tape full of love songs. He could be a complete wimp could Otway, but some of these songs like 'Can't Complain' were lovely. 'Geneve' sent a shiver down my spine the first time I heard it."

'Can't Complain' shows John's ability to portray the practicalities of romance:

> I looked in my atlas to see where you were
> I saw St. Julien, you were very near there
> I went to the travel agent to find out the fare
> She said it's 57 by train
> And 107 by air.

And balance it with the real emotion:

> Now my friends they all talk about the same things
> I'm sure they don't know what true loving is
> 'Cause when I kissed you honey I saw all the things
> Like stars and lights and rainbows ends.

'Geneve' is more like the 40-page letter only a great deal shorter, a song in which he attempts to impress on her his ambitions and plans for the future:

> *For she is so young and my dreams*
> *Are going to see me playing for the screaming ladies*
> *of Los Angeles*
> *And when I decided that would be my stage*
> *I was her age*
> *I remember that was a tender time for me.*

And as the spurned lover Otway writes:

> *For I am still young and it's true*
> *That I don't forget and I don't regret and I ain't going to*
> *And as I wipe away all the traces of Lisa blues*
> *It is my shoes*
> *That walk across the stage for the applause.*

A couple of years later he would have one final opportunity to impress her, and probably ruin his one chance of real stardom. As Potter says: "Love for Otway was a double-edged sword. It made him creative and gave him inspiration, but it also made him act in the most ridiculous ways at the same time."

CHAPTER
14

One thing happened that changed the whole music business and paved the way for Otway's success. The Sex Pistols had used the F-word very effectively on live TV, and made the combination of being shocking and playing badly very fashionable, a combination that was Otway's speciality. This had not escaped Willy's attention, and so he suggested to Otway that perhaps they should get a band together properly.

"I've just been playing around with this electric guitar, and I've got a few ideas that might work," he said. The electric guitar Willy had been playing around with was an astonishing contraption that dated back to the early sixties when the first electric guitars became popular. Willy's father had been interested in these instruments and had bolted a piece of scaffold plank to a Spanish guitar neck, then hacked the scaffolding around to the approximate shape he had seen on Hank Marvin's guitar on TV.

Ten years later Willy discovered this prototype instrument, finished it off, and named it the 'Les Dawson'. It had a sound of its own, and was to be his main instrument for the whole time he worked with Otway.

Willy had also discovered that through a heavy distortion pedal, a slide guitar could sound like a racing car, so he built a chassis and some wheels for it (so it could be ridden around the stage) and got Otway to write a song about fast vehicles to go with it. Jeff Potter had just passed his driving test and bought an old VW Beetle car. Now he could drive, he was calling himself Jet Spotter. The song 'Racing Cars' (Jet Spotter Of The Track) was dedicated to him and his girlfriend and contained the immortal lines "OK, I'm past the line. It's 69 with Magenta DeVine."

Willy cobbled up an electric banjo and an electric fiddle to go with everything else, and with this fine array of instruments went off to find some musicians. The musicians he found were Paul Kendall on bass and Edgar Rowe on drums.

That band for its short life was called John Otway And The Goatriders In Disguise, after their opening number 'Ghost Riders In The Sky'.

There is a pub called The Red Lion, in a place called Heath And Reach near Leighton Buzzard which is famous for no other reason than it was at this time the local of Barron Anthony. Barron was the founder member of The Barron Knights, a comedy/parody group who had hits in the sixties and seventies. The Red Lion was one of the few places to ever see this new Otway Barrett band.

The night they played in the pub there were five people in the audience. Twenty per cent of this audience was Barron himself.

He liked the crazy Otway, and he liked the fact that although there were only five people watching, Otway was still prepared to half-kill himself, wreck his equipment and vandalise the stage. After the show, Barron said he would like to help them out.

"Although it's not really my style," he told them, "I could probably get you some studio time to record your songs, and I know a couple of places that I might be able to get you some gigs."

The couple of places to get gigs didn't really work out, but the studio time was a blessing. "He really helped us out in a practical way," says John, "Both in getting the studio time, and as producer."

These recordings, along with the Townshend-produced material, gave Otway and Barrett eight well-recorded songs, enough to make up a good representative tape to send to record companies.

As we have found out, it is hard enough for Otway and Barrett to work with each other, never mind anyone else, and after a couple of weeks, four gigs and some recordings, Otway and Barrett ended up a duo again.

John at this point seriously considered getting a bone put through his nose. "Not a huge bone," he says seriously, "but a nice gold bone, a bit like a small chicken drumstick, in 18-carat gold. No one, not even Magenta, had anything that outrageous in Aylesbury, and it would have drawn attention to me. I mean you know what kids are like, they would have pointed me out to their mums and asked questions like 'Mummy, why has that man got a bone through his nose?' and things like that. All the local papers promised to do features if I had the nose job done, with headlines like 'The Man With The Golden Bone'".

Barron Anthony stupidly asked his doctor if he could do it and was told: "I have spent years in training to save lives and stop suffering. I feel my life could be more rewarding if I dedicated it to helping others. You are asking me if I will put a bone through someone's nose. Excuse me, can't you see I'm busy, perhaps you would save us all some time if you come back when you feel ill."

Eventually John's dentist, who had just given him 17 fillings, said he could probably make the bone and perform the necessary operation. He was planning to make the bone in two halves that screwed together, "so it wouldn't be too uncomfortable if I had a cold" says Otway.

By now, three of John's sisters were nurses, and the fourth was a social worker. In addition, his mum was teaching mentally handicapped children and his father was an ambulance driver. They were as a family all united and most definitely anti-bone. They were also by now fully aware that telling John it was a stupid idea was tantamount to encouragement. So in order to dissuade him from getting the operation performed, they managed to get any girl they knew John liked to say she wouldn't fancy him with a bone. This in fact wasn't difficult at all, as it was such a blatantly obvious result of the intended facial decoration. In the end, John's desire for desire beat his desire for notoriety, and the bone through the nose never happened.

"I still wish I'd have gone through with that sometimes, even now. It would have looked so good. I even had someone to design me a bone that curled round and had a pair of sunglass lenses on the top. I do have the nose to suit something like that. It was totally original, even through the days of punk, I never saw anything like that."

One day on the dustbins, Dave Crispin the driver told John, "You've been here a couple of years. It's a funny job this, if you don't get out now you'll probably be here until you retire."

Otway was thunderstruck. The whole idea of doing a job 'til he retired' was not only abhorrent, it went totally against his whole belief in his destiny. The next day he handed in his notice and vowed that he would never get another job.

On his last week on the bins, John found amongst the rubbish an old duplicator which he managed to restore in his father's shed.

"It's funny when you find something like that, it triggers off all sorts of thought patterns and things. I suddenly realised that

I could print my own magazines and newsletters and write to hundreds of record companies at the same time," says Otway. All of which he subsequently did.

Most of his last week's wages were spent on paper, ink, and postage, and an enormous volume of material was published from that shed in Ash Grove in the few weeks after June 25, 1976.

The first thing to be published was the *John Otway Newsletter*, an occasional sheet that has continued periodically since then. John went through his address book and dug out all the people that were interested in the progress of his career, and sent them a duplicated sheet, with details of gigs coming up, what he was doing recording-wise etc. His initial list was 20 people including his Aunt Agnes and Potter's sister, as well as Pete Townshend and a couple of more useful music people. Over the next few years, he would collect addresses at gigs at the end of the night and add others to the list, until it got to the four hundred it stands at today.

Thinking that one had to be original and inventive to get a record deal, John and Willy thought up a plan with which to approach all the record companies in the land, a total of 193.

"We only need a success rate of just over half a percent," Otway told Barrett – who could have replied that for this idea half a percent was unrealistically optimistic, but reality played no part in the following scheme, and all 193 record companies received letters hot from John's duplicator.

The first letter informed them that in five weeks time a tape would be sent to their company. They were told that they were competing with all the other British record companies to sign up the artists on the tape.

For the next five weeks, they received further letters telling them more about this competition they were entering into. A star would be drawn on the top of each letter. "Collect all five stars and send them in along with your offer of a record deal. The company who, in our opinion, offers the most money wins," it said.

Until the fifth letter and the tape were dispatched, no mention was made of who these 'mystery artists' might be.

"Just think," John said to Willy, "All these companies will be really curious as to who we are. As far as they know we could already have loads of gold records. They are bound to collect the stars in case they miss out on anything big. I wonder just how many collect the stars and how many of those send us an offer."

As far as we know, no one collected the stars. "I know for certain that no one sent us an offer," says John.

Following the failure of this bid to get a record deal, John had another idea. He knew that Track Records owned the copyright to the single 'Murder Man' and that they were also one of the very few useful people on his newsletter list. He planned a trick that would take several weeks to do, but might stand some chance of success.

He wrote to the 25 people on his newsletter list saying that he could, if sent a cassette, send back a copy of the material he and Willy had recorded.

In the next newsletter these people read that John had been inundated with hundreds of cassettes and was now staying up 'til four am copying cassettes in order to fulfil his fans' appetite for his music.

The following newsletter had the following: "This is all getting out of hand. If I'm going to be making up five hundred copies of these recordings on my two cassette machines by hand, I might as well do the job properly and get records made, as there is obviously the demand."

After that newsletter, John rang Track Records. "Er yes, John Otway here, I just wanted to check that you would let the copyright go on the tracks you own. That way I could release them on a little label for a few fans I have."

It worked; just occasionally Otway got it right and one of his schemes actually worked. They had read his newsletters and believed that somewhere in the home counties, thousands of Otway fans wanted his records.

"Look, I'm not trying to rip you off," John told Track, "You can always release the records yourself. It's just that if all those people want my music, it's my responsibility as an artist to make sure that it's available to them."

John and Willy were called in for a meeting and Track agreed that they would release the Pete Townshend-produced 'Louisa On A Horse'.

CHAPTER 15

Willy was right to get together with Otway at this time, fashion had indeed changed. Audiences now expected bands to sound bad. They came to be shocked, to gob at the bands and to pogo. Pogoing was very simple: you hopped up and down with both feet in or out of time to the music. Oddly enough it was a very good dance to do to Willy's bluegrass fiddle and banjo playing, which was now heavily amplified and put through a distortion pedal.

Most other punk acts were new to the idea of throwing themselves at the audience, banging their heads against microphones and damaging themselves and their equipment simultaneously. Otway had a head start on them all, he'd been doing it for years and needed no practice at the new art of being wild and shocking.

And so all of a sudden live work was no problem for the wild duo. They even started getting paid for the gigs: not a great deal, but a little more than Chris France was paying them for his local gigs. They started travelling further afield, and picked up strong followings in places like Luton, Oxford and Bognor Regis. "We're big in Bognor," Otway used to say after their first successful show there.

The music press also started taking a bit of interest, as the focus of attention had shifted from the big stadium and festival acts to the small up-and-coming punk acts that were now packing small pubs up and down the country.

As things improved and their profile increased, Otway and Barrett managed to put together a tour of Scotland, about six dates in all. This was their first proper tour. As their van was in a state guaranteed to get them no further north than Hemel Hempstead, Willy went looking for a vehicle suitable for a proper rock and roll tour and also capable of completing the journey.

He finally found one at a school in St. Albans – a 20-year-old, 22-seater coach for the amazingly small sum of £50. This was cheap and well within the budget they had allowed for transport. It was cheap for a reason and the headmaster of the school seemed well happy with the £50.

The part of Willy's character that made him quite happy to work with Otway (sometimes) was also the part that made him quite happy to take on other disasters and that coach was one of them. But Willy loved that coach: he bought aircraft seats for it, built two bedrooms in it and even ripped out all the cabinets, sink and cooker from the flat he was living in to try and make it into the perfect rock and roll tour bus.

As soon as they embarked on the tour, just after Hemel Hempstead in fact, the first problems with the coach became apparent. It wouldn't start.

"One was used to bump-starting all of Willy's vehicles," says John. "He never seemed to be able to get a car or a van that would start and you always ended up pushing them to get them going. Pushing a coach was hell, especially if it was the wrong way on a hill. You can ask passers-by to help push a car, try asking them to push a coach. In the end Willy got these two six-foot crow-bars that we could fit into the holes in the front wheels of the coach and literally crow-bar it up the hill, so we could push it down and try and get it going.

"One night after a gig we had to do that three times before the thing started. I went to bed almost in tears, not because I was upset but because my whole body ached from pushing the coach around.

"Willy had this idea that the coach would be good to bring back girls to, but the only time we ever managed it, they made excuses to leave as soon as Willy asked if they could help push."

Whether it was the extra physical exertion or nerves from doing his first tour, we don't know, but by the second date Otway had completely lost his voice. What John found surprising, though few others did, was that this did not affect the success of the tour. Otway was just as funny trying to sing as he was singing.

"There would be a bit of playing, followed by a little croaking noise. Willy would often slap my head and say, 'You're not trying hard enough,' so the croak would get a little louder," says John. "I suppose it was funny, but Willy managed to keep up the humour for a full hour show."

The night they played Edinburgh University a student, unaware of how bad this new punk music was supposed to sound, threw a plastic glass at Willy during the second number.

Willy's reactions were like lightning. He removed his banjo and, holding it like a tennis racquet in one hand, managed to lob the glass right back to the person who threw it. It was a brilliant piece of timing and Willy got the sort of standing ovation Centre Court players dream of.

The problem was that having seen the standard of play possible on that stage, the audience wanted to see more. At the end of each subsequent number there would be a burst of applause, followed by a barrage of glasses.

"We did our best to bat them all back," says Otway, "But there were far too many of them. We got hit on the head by a lot of glasses, which was a bit painful, but it was the only time I've been bottled off stage and gone down well at the same time."

Since the batch of songs from the Lisa episode John had not written a thing, and Potter and France were worried. They thought that those songs signalled a productive period from him. This was not to be. Months passed and there were no new songs at all. Potter figured it out.

"It's because he has no girlfriend to screw him up at the moment," he told Chris. "We ought to do something about this as it seems to be affecting his creativity."

Their opportunity came after an Aylesbury gig, one night while John's parents were on holiday. As usual, Otway turned Ash Grove into an open house the moment his folks had left. At the end of the night's show he walked on stage to thank the audience for coming and invited them all back to his place for a party.

At about two am that night, John was tired and decided to go to bed. "Don't let me spoil the party," he said going upstairs, "I'll see any of you who are still around when I get up in the morning."

Jeff and Chris got talking to a French girl called Marie. She was just over from France for a short holiday. It was her first time abroad and she was over here trying to improve her English, which was almost non-existent. She did, however, manage to get across to them that she liked the crazy singer a lot and that it was a shame that he had gone to bed.

"I'll show you where his room is then," said Potter, "And you can just climb into bed with him."

Somehow, the pair of them managed to convince this young lady that, in Britain, it was customary to just walk into a bedroom and climb into bed with someone if you happened to quite like them. And no, John would not think it at all unusual, he would take it as a compliment.

Having persuaded her that this behaviour was quite in order, they led her up to John's room and pushed her through the door.

"I was absolutely staggered" says John. "I woke up when the door opened and this girl I had never seen before walks in, takes all her clothes off, and climbs into bed with me."

Chris and Jeff waited outside the door for a few seconds until they heard the tell-tale sounds of passion and walked away congratulating themselves on a job well done. They well knew Otway's habit of falling for people who fell for him and this girl had certainly fallen for him. Not only that, she was going back to France shortly and he was bound to be heartbroken and write more songs.

"Marie was lovely," remembers John. "She was so sweet, I spent the few days she had left in Britain showing her around Aylesbury, and trying to teach her a bit of English. I suppose Potter and France were right, I was really sad when she left. I never let on to them though that I kept writing to her for the next six months. She did come back over for a few weekends after that, which was really nice. And yes I did write a few Marie songs but I don't want Potter and France to know which ones they are. They've had too much of a laugh over that story as it is, and I really liked Marie."

The Oranges And Lemons pub in Oxford can easily claim to have witnessed more Otway and Barrett gigs than anywhere else. In one twelve-month period the duo played this place fifty times. It was one of the few places in Oxford where the students mixed freely with the rest of the town's population and celebrated this new aggressive music.

Otway loved the place: it was where he and Willy had knocked their act into a workable form in front of a very appreciative audience. The crowd there were also very faithful, and if a coach was arranged for them they would travel miles to come and support the duo. The Oranges And Lemons was also where John met a young attractive blonde girl called Paula Yates. She was at college in Oxford and must have been fascinated enough by Otway to ask him out.

After his date with Paula it was love again. John went around telling everyone he knew about this wonderful girl he had met, and how he was going to see her in a couple of days. He asked advice from them about what he should wear, which earrings to put in and whether or not he should get a haircut.

Paula, having been fascinated enough to ask him out, was not fascinated enough to put up with another evening with him and stood him up.

"It's the last time she'll ever get the chance to go out with a Rock Star," Otway complained bitterly.

CHAPTER
16

When Track released 'Louisa On A Horse', it was immediately apparent that there were not thousands of Otway fans desperate for Otway product. The sales figures of the record show that a few more copies were sold than the number of addresses on John's newsletter list but, as most of us know, 50 record sales do not make a hit.

Before these sales had time to register though, the powers-that-be at Track came to see a live show. It was time to pull out all the stops. The show they chose was at The Roundhouse in London, where Otway and Barrett fans could not be counted on one hand – because there were none. Coaches were laid on from Oxford, Luton, Aylesbury and Bognor Regis, and Otway printed up a thousand handouts to give out at all the gigs to advertise the fact that they really needed help on this.

"He was good at getting us all on his side," an old Oxford fan remembers. "He used to say things like: 'Now when I do this gig, I know you don't know the song, but if you can get everybody to applaud loudly when I sing the first line of the third song, as if it's one of your favourites, that'll really impress the record company.' So sure enough he sings the first line, and he's got the whole audience at it, he sings one line of this song no one's heard before and the place is going bananas and it's a couple of minutes before he can carry on with the song. We all used to go along with things like that, 'cause it was as if we were in on something. It was good to watch the bemused faces of these music biz people."

"Yeah, I remember doing that," says John, "It was a good laugh. They'd come up to you afterwards and tell you how much they liked the third number we did."

Track Records were impressed by the show and still felt they were on to a good thing. Willy used this opportunity to persuade them to buy a van for their new artistes. "You can't have your new stars pushing a coach to every gig," Willy explained. And so they managed to get a blue two-year-old ex-police transit, the first decent transport they had ever owned. It even looked quite smart – but not for long.

In the Track offices Otway spotted a badge making machine in the corner. "Cor, can I borrow that to make some Otway badges?" he asked excitedly, and so over the next few gigs many a punter would be wearing a badge that said, "I liked John Otway even before he was a Star". Far fewer were wearing the alternative "Wouldn't it be nice to go to bed with Otway" though.

When the record finally came out, Track realised that sales would not recoup the cost of pressing them, let alone pay for a new van. They quite liked their new signing however, and decided to keep them on for a while. They felt they might have heard something in the Otway and Barrett repertoire that could just be a hit record.

"It's about time we made an LP," the duo told Track. "We can't afford to do an LP when you're only selling 50 records." "That's because I'm probably an album artist," John told them. "Rubbish," they said. "Look, we'll give you the money for the studio time to make a single. We suggest you do that 'Really Free' song, it sounds catchy and more like a hit record than anything else you've got."

"That song is not a hit record," Otway told Willy as they drove home in the new van. "'Racing Cars' is more like a hit, you know how the audiences go wild when you ride around on the slide guitar and crash it at the end of the song. Now that is a hit."

They got Barron Anthony to produce 'Racing Cars' for them and took it back to the record company. "We thought you were going to record 'Really Free'," Track said when Otway and Barrett played them their new recording. "This might be a great live number, but it is not a hit record. Go away and think again."

Meanwhile Track had started getting them higher profile gigs in London. The main one of these was at The Speakeasy Club in Margaret Street, in the heart of the West End, whose clientèle was made up of music business people – from record companies and agents to stars and disc jockeys and the odd drunk music journalist. Most of the bands that played there were more or less ignored by those who frequented the place and so, as a gig, it was not thought of as the greatest place in the world to play.

However it was almost impossible to ignore Otway and Barrett, and if you did, you did so at your peril. It was quite likely that Otway's size 11 shoes would be standing in your very expensive pint of lager as he leapt four feet onto your table, or you got hit in the eye by a flying button from the shirt he was ripping open.

Some of the people who saw Otway and Barrett there were to play a large role in this story and affect their career. One of these was Tony Bramwell, who was working for Polydor Records, and another was Jeff Griffen, the producer of both the BBC's *In Concert* on radio and *The Old Grey Whistle Test* on TV. Pete Townshend came down to see the pair of them playing at The Speakeasy, and ended up a little worse for wear. He wrote the song 'Who Are You' after his experiences that night.

The situation with Track records was getting worse. Otway and Barrett were as adamant about doing an LP as Track were adamant about them doing 'Cor Baby That's Really Free', and then, if that went well, think about an album. John and Willy decided to go and record an album anyway and take the finished thing back to the record company. "They'll see I'm right about being an album artist when they hear it," John said.

Apart from the four Townshend-produced tracks, the rest of that first album was recorded at Chalk Farm studios in February 1977. When it was finally handed in to Track the following month, Track had had enough.

"You can keep the van, you can have the rights back to the tracks we own, the only thing we want back is the badge making machine." they were told, and Otway and Barrett realised that their record company were just as adamant as they were about the LP.

So there they were with a finished LP and no record company. "I'd borrowed a lot of money from Chris France and people like that to pay for the studio time," says John. "I'd told them it was all right as they would get the money back from Track Records as soon as we had handed in the tape, so it was a bit embarrassing to get fired from them and having to tell everybody that they'd just have to wait."

John and Willy decided that the only course of action was to follow their normal tradition of solving problems: by borrowing even more money and putting the LP out themselves.

The figures involved were high. To do the LP properly, they would need to borrow £6,000, which would mean John's total debt to date would be over £10,000.

In the end John's father agreed to re-mortgage the house in order to finance the record. His parents had by now completely given up hope that their son would ever do anything sensible for a living. He was working about two nights a week with Willy, and was at last actually getting paid for doing what he really liked.

"It could be worse," they thought to themselves, "He could be a criminal or a drug addict. He's a cheerful optimistic boy and has worked hard at doing this – he even had his record played on the radio once or twice." They even felt a bit sorry for him getting fired from his first proper record company after working so hard to make a record for them.

Otway and Barrett decided to call their new record label Extracked because they were now ex-Track. The album was given the very original title of 'John Otway And Wild Willy Barrett', and the album artistes set about the task of organising labels, pressings and sleeves.

The thing that takes the longest in record production is in fact the sleeves – the printing of these can take anything up to a month. John and Willy are not the most patient of people and worked out that they could halve this waiting period by using self adhesive stickers on plain white sleeves. Even though this meant sticking four thousand stickers on two thousand LPs by hand they both felt it was worth it to save a fortnight's wait.

The media in general are well aware of how badly artists are treated by record companies and how often these sensitive creative people are either ripped off or mistreated by the men with money. The case of Otway and Barrett being fired by their company attracted a great deal of sympathy from both the press and the radio.

Small independent labels forming to release the music the big record companies would not touch was just starting to happen. 1977 was punk's biggest year, and the major labels had no idea which bands to sign, they all sounded awful. When major labels tried to pick an awful band themselves they invariably picked the wrong one.

On the release of their first LP, John and Willy managed to get features in *Melody Maker* and *Sounds*, and reviews on several radio programmes, as well as news items on the new label and the 'fired from Track' story. Jeff Griffen, to help get them underway with the new label, gave them a Radio One *In Concert* programme, which was broadcast the day after the album was released.

This was major publicity for the duo and its effect on sales was dramatic. John's father, who had just retired, took to selling by phone and sold five hundred. A couple of record distributors got in touch and the first batch of two thousand LPs was sold within a week.

"There were times over those few weeks," says John, "That I wished we'd waited for the sleeves to be printed. We ended up sticking something like eight thousand stickers on those LPs in about three weeks.

Extracked records only lasted a month. It was one of the very first independent labels in the country, but this small company with one successful record was soon to be involved in a takeover bid by one of the biggest companies in the land.

CHAPTER 17

Tony Bramwell was the record plugger at Polydor. He had taken an interest in the duo after seeing them at The Speakeasy and, as Polydor distributed Track Records, he had helped get some radio play for 'Louisa'. He was also on Otway's newsletter list.

Tony liked the album, it was raw and energetic and it was doing well both in sales and radio play. He called John and Willy into Polydor and with the A&R man Chris Parry, worked out a deal which gave an advance of £15,000. And yes, Polydor would release 'Racing Cars' as the next single.

Giving Otway, or even Barrett for that matter, large sums of money always guarantees a good story, so here goes.

Now he was a recording star on a big label, John felt he had outgrown his home town. Yes, it had been good to him and supported him while he was making his first steps on the ladder to fame, but as he was nearing the top of that ladder, the time had come to move to the big city where the action was.

He had also met Kathy Archbold. She was a blonde-haired artist, a couple of years older than himself, who he desperately wanted to live with. Kathy didn't mind the idea of living with John, but she didn't want him moving into her bedsit. So John had to find a flat.

Anyone who has tried to rent a flat in London knows how difficult it can be. It can take weeks of searching and fortunes in cabs tearing around London, only to be beaten by someone else doing the same thing. John was now a recording star, and it took him a day. He had spotted a flat in Fulham advertised in the *Evening Standard*, for a short six-month let. He phoned Kathy, would she live in Fulham? On getting the affirmative, Otway tore round to the flat in a cab.

"I'll have it," he said to the chap as he answered the door. "But don't you want to see it?" "OK then," said John, "But quickly as I'm very busy. I'm a recording artist on Polydor Records."

"Yes it's fine," said Otway as he poked his head through each door of the small flat. "But I've got other people coming to see it, and I need bank references and the like to make sure you can pay the rent every month and it will take a couple of weeks," said the landlord.

Otway didn't want to wait long at all. He didn't want anyone else looking at it either – they might have more sensible jobs like accountants or stockbrokers – and if someone like that wanted the flat, Otway was sure that this chap was going to give it to them.

As he was thinking all this, he saw a cab with a bank manager type getting out. "Don't give the flat to anyone else 'till I get back," he said rushing out of the door. "I'll be back in 10 minutes."

Ten minutes later, he was back on the doorstep clutching £1,500. "Here's the whole six months' rent in advance," said John. "You won't need bank references, so can I have the flat now?"

Otway's new landlord was delighted at the deal. He was off on a long holiday, and the thought of being able to take all the rent money away with him pleased him a great deal. So yes, John could have the flat and he could move in tomorrow if he liked.

"You did what?" said Kathy when he called to tell her the good news about her new home. "And that's about twice the rent for flats in that area." she said when he told her how much it cost.

"You mean to tell me that you didn't even get a receipt for the £1,500 you handed over in cash?" she asked incredulously.

"Oh my god, well how many rooms has it got?"

"What do you mean, you think it's got one bedroom?"

"Don't you think that I might have wanted to see our new home before you got it?"

On this note, at the age of 24, John left home and moved into Lambrook Terrace with Kathy. And so, for a few years, Ash Grove became a quieter, if less eventful place to live.

Getting the advance also meant that John and Willy could employ a full-time roadie, and could get a car rather than travel in the van. No one wanted to travel in the van any more, as it was a horrendous pink colour. The reason was Otway's superstition.

While in Weymouth, he went to see a fortune teller on the sea front. As he sat down, expecting to be told how famous he was going to be, the lady looked at him and said, "You've got a blue van."

Otway's mouth fell open. "I don't think it's very lucky for you," she said. And that was it, the next day John stood over Barrett and made him paint it with the only paint Willy had, some bright pink gloss he had bought to paint the door in his new flat.

John couldn't drive, he still can't. When he left school, he had bought himself a motorbike – which caused great concern among his family and friends.

"The law about wearing crash helmets was passed with people like Otway in mind," says Potter. "In his 14 days as a biker his crash helmet saved his life seven times."

With a record like that, neither he, nor anyone else, wanted him to drive, so the car was down to Willy. Willy picked a Jaguar XJ12, a monster of a car that could, and often did, go at 140 mph.

Otway enjoyed living in London. Moving there started the most exciting year of his life so far and certainly the most successful. Most days, he would go into Polydor and pester them. When one department of the company got sick of him hanging around, he would move onto the next. First the press department, then the art department, then sales. "Blimey, he puts more hours in this building than anyone who works here," one company employee remarked.

One day, the telephone sales department got so fed up with him hanging around, that they gave him a telephone and a list of shops to call. He spent the day ringing them, and asking how many Otway and Barrett records they wanted to buy that week.

Chris Parry, the A&R man at Polydor, introduced John to a publisher, Bryan Morrison. Bryan was a force to be reckoned with in the music business. He managed and published Pink Floyd for a while, as well as other huge acts in the sixties, and had just signed The Jam for publishing. He was intrigued by this whole new punk movement, and could smell a hit in this 'Really Free' song, so he signed John for publishing, giving him another few thousand pounds to play with.

Paul Kendall was leaving University that year, and John needed a manager to help him with his new situation. Nothing in Paul's education had prepared him for the job Otway was asking him to do, which in a nutshell was: "I want you to curb my excesses and make sure that I don't do anything stupid." Paul Kendall was looking for a challenge, but had he known then what he knows now, he would probably have used a large wooden mallet as opposed to intelligent reasoning to achieve his goals.

'Racing Cars' was not a hit. It did sell marginally more than 'Louisa', but it came and went in much the same way as the previous single.

Bryan Morrison was used to dealing with artistes, he understood their egos, their sensitivity, their vulnerability and their genius. He was also remarkably good at getting hit records out of them.

"Otway, you're being bloody stupid – that 'Really Free' song is a hit." Pointing to each one of the gold and platinum records adorning his walls, he said "I've got a lot of these, you haven't, and there's a damn good reason. I don't go around acting like a prat. Now for God's sake go and record a decent version of that song. I like successful records, even if you don't."

For some reason this speech, or rather tirade, seemed to get through to John, who said to Paul Kendall, "Do you think he's got a point?" And it finally dawned on Paul Kendall just what a challenge this sort of job was for a young graduate.

There was a version of 'Really Free' on the LP, but it was not particularly powerful. Bryan wanted it to sound 'ballsy' and 'brash' – more like the current hits at the time. At The Oranges And Lemons in Oxford, Willy heard a completely outrageous punk band called Ken Liversausage who were exactly that, ballsy and brash. They were also brilliantly shocking with a touch of appalling theatrical humour: their songs had titles like 'Gooseberry Puss', and the lead singer was planning to have a vasectomy performed on himself live on stage, while the band played behind. They had an amazing rhythm section, using two drummers, who hammered out the fast punk beat in a wall of sound that would have impressed Phil Spector.

Willy liked this group. They appealed to his taste for anything diabolical and he took them into the studio to record a few of their most obnoxious numbers. Whilst producing the band, Willy got the drummers to record the drums for the two numbers 'Really Free' and 'Beware Of The Flowers'. He then recorded the other instruments himself and finally added Otway's voice.

"It's brilliant," said Bryan when he heard it. "It's horrible," muttered Otway to Barrett. "Well I don't have to take responsibility for this one." (Later he would go back on this, and take full responsibility).

And so, a release date of November 5 was set for the release of 'Cor Baby That's Really Free', and the great wheels of the Polydor machine were set in motion for another Otway and Barrett release.

Tony Bramwell had managed to get Otway and Barrett a couple of TV spots to promote the single. The first was a regional programme called *So It Goes* filmed in Manchester, and the second was an appearance on the *Old Grey Whistle Test*.

"Let's not do 'Really Free'," John said to Willy on their way up to Manchester, "Let's do something better." Which they did. (Not something better, something else.)

"Why the Hell didn't you play your single on the telly?" Tony Bramwell fumed. "I got you those things to help promote your record."

"He has a point," said Paul Kendall, "I bet Bryan Morrison isn't too happy either." And Paul was right.

So John and Willy backed down and promised to do their new single on the forthcoming *Old Grey Whistle Test*. They did two numbers on that programme, 'Really Free' and 'Cheryl's Going Home'.

John was nervous. It was his first time on national television and as always in these situations, he was more wild and unpredictable than usual. There were the normal somersaults with the guitar and the ripping of the shirt, but Otway was really going for it. Willy's amplifier was set up on a chair in the studio and during 'Cheryl's Going Home', Otway made a daring five-foot leap on to it, in order to deliver a couple of lines from a more elevated position. But he slipped. One leg slipped over one side of the amplifier, and the other leg slipped over the other. The full weight of the leaping Otway hammered down in the direction of the most delicate parts of his body.

The results of this were two-fold. Willy's amplifier got ripped out of the socket in the wall, so silencing the only source of music, and Otway was rolling around the floor in agony unable to carry on singing.

"No one had ever done anything like that live on television before," says John, "Especially not on a serious rock programme. Eventually the roadies managed to plug Willy back in and we finished the song, though Willy did occasionally remind me of the lyrics. In the end, Willy looked so cross that we left the stage in opposite directions."

The effect of that appearance was instantaneous. The following day they played at a club expecting the usual hundred people, and five hundred turned up. Sales of 'Really Free', which had been selling about 20 per day, started selling two hundred, and within a week John Otway and Wild Willy Barrett were in the charts.

CHAPTER 18

Most people would agree that having worked so long and hard to get a successful act together, falling out the moment you have some real success is not the wisest course of action. But that is what John and Willy proceeded to do.

The first signs of a tiff came when Willy dropped John off on the M1 at three am. "It was our car, we'd paid half each. Willy had said that he would drive me home to London after a gig in Manchester and then he dropped me off on the Northampton turn-off on the M1. It's the hardest place in the world to hitch a lift from. He said he was tired or something. I couldn't see why I should have to pay for half the car if I was going to have to hitch-hike back from gigs."

Willy wanted to get on and record the next LP and single, so that they would have something to follow up 'Really Free'. John wanted to go out and do a tour... "because lots of people will come and see us now that we've got a hit record."

In the end Willy started recording the next LP and John did a deal with a local group called Scratch, to back him on a solo tour.

Willy did of course do the TV appearances that came up, which were a *Sight And Sound In Concert* for the BBC and two appearances on *Top Of The Pops* as their single soared up to 27 in the charts.

They were good times though. Otway would love going on stage and saying "We are now going to play our hit record." He went into Polydor as often as he could, grinning like a child and saying "It is a hit before Christmas." Although this sort of showing off might be unpleasant in some people, it came as a refreshing change that someone who showed off so much actually had something to show off about.

John's parents were pleased, Chris France rang his bank manager to give him the good news and Jeff Potter's faith in destiny was, for a while, well rewarded. Christmas 1977 was the best Christmas ever, one in which John could actually afford to buy his family presents. He and Kathy decorated the Fulham flat with a picture of Otway on the top of the Christmas tree instead of a star.

Otway and Barrett had recorded a concert at The Roundhouse over the Summer. John pressed up 250 records from the tapes, and sent them out as a limited edition as presents to the people on his newsletter list. He also bought a bottle of champagne to be opened to celebrate the next hit.

The tour with Scratch was successful. People in their hundreds turned out to see if Otway was going to do himself as much of an injury at the performances as he had on TV.

Things in the studio were not going quite so well though. The first LP had been comparatively easy, as there was all the material John had ever written to pick from. For this album there was not the same kind of choice.

"With Otway," says Willy, "there was always a wealth of really wimpy love songs, but never enough good up-tempo things that would make good singles. When I gave him a bit of a hard time about this, he'd just say, 'How about this,' and play one of his wimp songs faster."

Unlike the very first recording of 'Misty Mountain', where the lyrics of the song were not completed until Otway had reached the studio, for a couple of the songs on this album, lyrics were not even completed when John was in front of the microphone expected to sing them. He made them up as he went along, hoping that no one would be able to tell the difference.

Otway had spotted the opportunity to record something on his own. He had never got over the fact that he was spurned by Lisa. Now he was no longer a dustman he felt that there was a way of making her feel that she had made a big mistake, and that he had been right all along about the 'screaming ladies of Los Angeles.' Otway had a flair for romance that flabbergasted everyone by its dramatic intensity and expense, rather than impress his intended suitor.

And so on the very last day of 1977 – John's most successful year – a one hundred-piece orchestra was booked, the Olympic studio was booked, David Soul's arranger was bought in to arrange and conduct the orchestra, and another Otway epic was underway.

"The really nice thing about that session," remembers John, "was standing up in front of that huge orchestra, on a rostrum next to the conductor, singing 'Geneve' live. I felt like a star then. It was the sort of thing that I had seen people like Frank Sinatra do and it was great to be able to do it myself. This'll show her I thought."

John had not told anyone he was doing this; Paul Kendall did not know, Willy did not know, Polydor did not know. In fact, the only people who had any clue at all about what he was up to were the 150-or-so people involved in the session itself. "It was a sort of intensely private personal gesture," John remarks.

"I've just had a go at recording another version of 'Geneve'," John commented to Paul Kendall as he was driving up the A40 back to London the day after the session. "Would you like to hear it?"

"The stupid bugger, I was expecting to hear a bit of a bad Otway demo, and this thing came on. We almost crashed three times."

The first crash nearly happened when the recording started, as the soft sweet strings played a quiet gentle introduction to the song. "I was shocked, but I just gripped the wheel and thought, 'Heavens above, he's used some string players," said Paul.

The first major swerve of the car came after the line 'I remember that was a tender time for me,' when the whole orchestra – strings, brass, and Timpani – crescendoed to the sort of peak Beethoven used to appreciate when he was deaf.

The time when the car almost went under an articulated lorry was on the part of the A40 known as Hanger Lane. It was just after John had sung the last bit of the song. There was a moment's pause, followed by a drum break, followed by the whole orchestra topped by a screaming electric guitar, all playing mezzo forte, followed by heavy braking on the part of Paul.

The final near-miss, and potentially the most catastrophic accident, came after Paul asked the question, "How on earth much did that cost?"

Even Willy, who was, more than anybody, used to Otway's excesses was shocked, and commented: "For heavens sake, we're supposed to be an outrageous punk act, and Otway goes out and records something that sounds more fitting in a Walt Disney film."

After that, this recording became known as the 'Walt Disney version' of 'Geneve', and the gap between the duo grew a little wider.

John and Willy had signed only a short contract with Polydor. They had bought the first LP off them and Otway and Barrett were only due to deliver one more.

In these days of punk music, the major labels worked on the principle that if an act had a hit record then it must be a good punk act, and if it didn't then it was a bad one. They had not had a great deal of success with this new music and the only other act that they had broken recently was The Jam.

So Polydor wanted to sign the duo to a long three-year contract, with a commitment to make four LPs. However, long before they had even met their obligations for the first contract, enough differences between the two parties of the duo had arisen to make negotiations very strange indeed.

It was now pretty obvious to Otway that he and Willy could not last forever. "We're after different things," he would say. "Willy's a musician, and I'm a star."

It is fair to say that neither Otway nor Barrett had the financial acumen of a businessman. Paul Kendall, who had, was endlessly overruled by Otway. John appeared to enjoy making his job of 'Otway's spending controller' as difficult as possible. In the end it was Bryan Morrison, who could impress John enough with his wall of gold records to listen to him, who eventually got the job of sorting out a deal that meant Otway and Barrett could record separately or together.

Every year at Cannes in the South of France, there is a music festival, similar to the film festival, called Midem. All areas of the international music business attend. That January, 1978, Polydor were there in force, and as guests of their record company, Otway and Barrett were invited.

Willy did not want to go as he preferred to finish off the LP. "It will be horrible," Willy said, "Full of people posing and drinking champagne, talking about what deals they are doing, and everybody trying to impress everybody else."

It was exactly as Willy supposed and this was exactly the reason why John wanted to go so badly. In the end he took Kathy, who got a little bored with John, who was horrible. He posed, he drank champagne, he talked about the deal he was doing, and did his best to impress everybody.

Bryan Morrison used this forum to sort out the deal with Polydor. He caught up with John and Kathy in the Martinez bar as John was finishing off his glass of Veuve Cliquot.

"This deal," he said, "will give you almost a quarter of a million over the next three years. Congratulations, you are rich."

"It's not enough," said Otway, who tried to explain to Bryan that he was destined for stardom. As he had only just had one hit, he was actually worth more. "Think of it this way. After I've had about 10 hits, I'm going to be worth more than that, and that's what I reckon one has in three years."

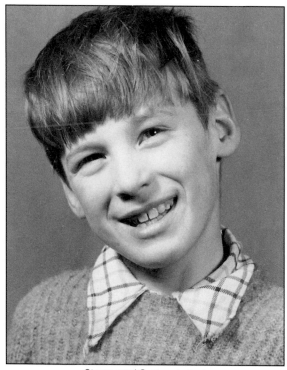

Otway, aged 8. *(Otway Archives)*

Jeff Potter (left) and teenage Otway.
(Martin Goddard)

Teenage Otway in love with Sue Reece.
(Otway Archives)

Jeff Potter, John Otway and Chris France around the time of the 'hit'.
(Issy Brampton)

Otway plays to his home town crowd in Aylesbury Market Square.
(The Bucks Herald)

Dwarfed by the big picture at the Reading Festival, 1978, with Maurice Bacon on drums. *(Clive Smith)*

The Otway account.

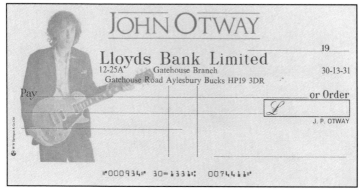

Drag night at the Red Cow in Hammersmith, 1978. Kathy Archbold applies the make-up for a unique Otway performance.
(London Features International)

Otway and Barrett live in Coventry.

Otway 'Live In A
Living Room' in East
Kilbride, 1979. *(Rick)*

Otway & Barrett
promo shot,
circa. 1980.

Otway hands over
the proceeds from
the Polython benefit
concert to Polydor
managing director
Tony Morris and his
chief accountant,
1980. *(Otway Archives)*

From riches to rags: before Maurice took over Otway's management (left) and after (right). *(left: Steve Emberton; right: Heidi Nery)*

John Otway amd Paul Bradley. *(John Breen)*

Otway with fellow actors Robert Morley and Will Lyman in a 1986 episode of *William Tell*. *(Otway Archives)*

Chris France, Otway's personal banker and loan shark, in 1989. *(Normanski)*

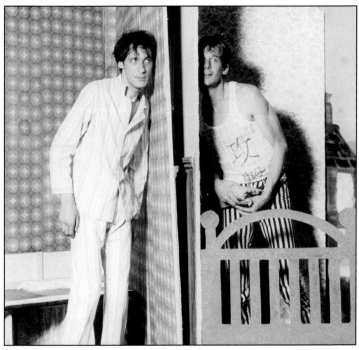

Otway and Simon Roberts in the play *Verbal Diary*.

Ronnie Caryl. *(Otway Archives)*

Robin Boult. *(Otway Archives)*

"But you've had one hit that's only got to 27 in the charts. I've got you nearly a quarter of a million pounds and you don't think it's enough?" Bryan asked bemused.

Bryan called over an American lawyer friend of his, whom he had used in the past to organise some multi-million pound American record deals. He explained the situation to the lawyer, and asked him what he thought. "How the hell did you get Polydor to offer that sort of money on an act like that?" was his instant reaction.

In the end, after convincing Otway that it really was the best he could do, John reluctantly agreed to go ahead with the deal.

On arrival back in England, John put the final vocals on the new LP, which was to be called 'Deep and Meaningless', and he and Willy prepared for their first tour together after the hit.

For this tour, they decided to hire extra musicians, and to go out as a band. These were the two drummers from Ken Liversausage, the bass player from Scratch, and an old friend of Willy's, Paul Ward, on keyboards.

It was to be far and away their most successful tour, and John loved every moment of it. Paul Kendall sorted out a good agent to book the dates, booked good hotels, and arranged for a new EMI band called The Flys to support them on the whole tour of the UK. They all went around the country happy and packing in the crowds.

As 'Really Free' was the only song that most of their new audience knew, rather than having the crowd yelling for it all the way through the show, they started their set with it and repeated it as the encore. The Flys, the support band, were employed to sing backing vocals on a couple of numbers, and Willy built a brand new formula-one style slide guitar with which to do 'Racing Cars'.

Willy had a new girlfriend Yvonne, who he had brought in to do backing vocals on the album. Willy invited her on tour, and emerged from his hotel room only to do the soundchecks and the shows.

Willy found it a little tiring that Otway had this habit of doing up to seven encores per night, and as soon as 'Really Free' was over as the encore, he would get into the XJ12 and head back to the hotel.

"I felt it was good to leave the audience on the high spot yelling and screaming for more," he says. "I couldn't see the point in doing what Otway was doing and go back on and do six more songs just 'cause they were still clapping."

"Willy just wanted to get back to the hotel," says John. "He was quite happy to leave the audience chanting for us, and wasn't willing to give them what they wanted. I'd have to go back on on my own without Willy to keep them happy."

By the end of that tour, the album was delivered to Polydor, and the new deal was sorted out. This meant that it was the only time Otway had large sums of money to deal with.

Paul Kendall had sorted out an accountant in Aylesbury to look after the new company, set up to deal with Otway's new-found wealth.

"I don't see why you need to take a black cab the 45 miles between Aylesbury and London just to see the accountant," Paul said. "Well I had to meet a couple of people and it was running late. I didn't think I'd make it in time, so I just hailed a cab in Oxford Street. I made it on time though, didn't I?"

The accountant informed John and Paul that they could afford to buy a car each to offset against their tax. "And that might mean you don't have to get cabs from London," he explained carefully.

Paul got a good deal on a one-year-old Ford Cortina Estate car, which was a pretty good compromise between a saloon, and something that could carry a fair amount of equipment. In all a pretty good manager's car.

Otway on the other hand had different needs to Paul, firstly he could not drive and secondly he was a star and not a manager.

The search for a star's car came to an end when John and Jeff spotted a 1949 Bentley driving through the streets of Mayfair. John did not know what it was at the time he just said, "That's really nice," to Potter and then spotted the 'For Sale' sign on the back window as it passed them.

"Chase that car and get that number," he yelled, and Potter chased the car on foot around Berkeley Square and up Bruton Street.

John needed someone to get the car for him and knew it would be pointless asking Paul Kendall, as he would refuse point blank to consider it.

"It was a lot easier to deal with Paul," says John, "if one did something extravagant and then told him the deed had been done, rather than explain to him first that you were going to do it."

Chris France was the obvious person to go and do the deal on the car. Chris had just got all the money back from John that he owed him, and was more than delighted to help him sort out the purchase.

Chris was even more delighted when he saw it, because it was a truly beautiful machine. As he sat on the leather upholstery, ran his hands over the walnut finishes, admired the handbuilt coachwork and marvelled at the stunning silver and black finish, it occurred to him, as Otway could not drive, someone else would have to, and what would John do with the car when he was not using it. Yes he thought, John has to buy this car.

The flat John and Kathy had in Fulham was not in the most exclusive street in that area of London, and one could not miss a shiny 1949 Bentley parked outside 33, Lambrook Terrace.

Paul Kendall noticed it the moment he turned off the Fulham Palace Road.

"Like my new car?" Otway enquired beaming as he let Paul in. "Better than a common old Cortina eh? And it was a bargain."

Paul was becoming resigned to the way Otway was reacting to stardom, and was reduced to just pointing out John's financial waywardness. All he could say was. "Otway, you could have lessened the shock a little by removing the 'For Sale' sign with the price on it out of the back window."

Over one of the many meals Otway had in one of the many expensive restaurants in London, Kathy told John the story of how Picasso would sign for his small bills and his signature was worth more than the amount being charged. In this way Pablo saved on things like his milk bill.

It was the sort of story that impressed Otway, and would trigger off an idea. "If I get some cheques printed up with a nice photo of myself on them," he thought, "I may do even better than Picasso. They would become collectors' items. The man on the corner shop could frame his Otway cheque and say to customers in years to come, 'Oh yes, John used to buy his Old Holborn tobacco in this shop when he lived around the corner.' I could get free tobacco, beer, food and newspapers, as well as milk."

The idea was classic Otway, and once he had thought it up, it was pretty obvious that it would come to fruition. And so a photo session was booked, special art work was commissioned, and John's bank manager, thankful that the letters O.D. did not appear after every entry in his statements for once, organised the printing. All in all pretty expensive.

"You'll need a lot of free tobacco, beer, food, newspapers and milk to recoup this little venture," Paul said wryly.

It was also time for John to start thinking of moving flat. "Why don't you buy one?" said Bryan Morrison, Paul Kendall, Chris France and most other people who knew Otway's financial status.

"Because I might find myself living in New York or Hollywood very soon. What I need is somewhere to tide me over for a few months and a few more hits," was his reply.

And so John found a very expensive flat in Randolph Avenue in a financial deal that meant him handing over £9,000 in cash. It made the deal for the Fulham flat almost look sensible.

"I liked it there a lot," says Otway. "The whole area was full of flats with famous people. Dave Stewart from the Eurythmics lived just down the road, Les Gray from Mud was my next door neighbour and Dave Edmunds lived in the house opposite.

John also found a local pub to replace The Derby Arms as headquarters for his schemes. A place where he could hang out with others, like himself, who had had hit records. It was Les Gray's local too and the pair of them soon became friends and drinking partners.

Now he had most things befitting a star: a suitable car, a suitable flat and a hit record. Otway decided he needed a press agent. "Someone needs to look after my press for me and make sure that I'm in the papers all the time," he insisted, and so Paul Kendall was given the job of finding a company to fulfil this position.

There were several press agents around, some of them were new young hungry companies who understood how to get press on those shocking young punk acts. Because they were new they were relatively inexpensive. There was also the older established agents who handled the press for people like Barbara Streisand, Shirley Bassey and Rod Stewart and as one can imagine, they were horribly expensive.

"But they are really the sort of press agent I need, and as my career takes off, they will understand how I work, and will do a better job. Look Paul, we didn't come all this way to go with a second-rate press agent, did we?"

And so Otway became a client of one of the most expensive and oldest press agents in the world. "See Paul, their main office is in Hollywood, and you know that I eventually want to move into films, don't you?"

In early that year of 1978, Capital Radio held its annual awards, and who should be nominated for the award for the most promising newcomer but Messrs Otway and Barrett. Willy did not wish to attend the ceremony for the usual posing and champagne reasons. John was more than happy to get Chris to chauffeur him in his new Bentley to the Savoy hotel. Sadly no one got to hear the acceptance speech he had written apart from Chris who had to put up with several hours of Otway rehearsing it.

"I could never work out why he'd never rehearse his show, but was quite happy to rehearse for something like this," Chris remarked at the time.

At the awards John got chatting to a couple who said they liked his single and were wishing him all the best with the next song. "This girl looks familiar he thought," and he went rushing back to his table to announce that he thought that someone famous liked his hit.

"Yes you're right, she is famous," someone from Polydor said as John later pointed them out to him. "The girl is Linda McCartney and the bloke you were talking to was Paul."

Anyhow, Capital Radio got things a bit right as Otway and Barrett were not the most promising newcomers that year, Tom Robinson was.

CHAPTER 20

The time had arrived to decide on the follow up single to 'Really Free'. Polydor could not find anything suitable on the new LP, 'Deep And Meaningless', and the general feeling was that the most suitable track would have been 'Beware Of The Flowers'. Sadly this had been used on the B-side of the last single.

Otway had played Polydor his epic version of 'Geneve', and was more than happy for that to be released as the follow up. "Its bound to be a hit after that last single," he thought. "Won't it be nice to be not only a great punk artist but a ballad singer as well."

He foresaw other advantages too. He had written the song in the first place to demonstrate his love for Lisa, and to impress on her that he would be a great star eventually, even if he was a dustman at the time – it would be her loss if she wasn't with him then. He had no idea where she was now, but he was certain that if 'Geneve' went climbing up the charts, reporters and photographers by the planeload would fly to Switzerland and find her. Then she would really know the pain of his unrequited love.

The song he felt was universal. "Anyone who had ever been spurned by the true desire of their heart would relate to this song."

His imagination ran wild. He could see pictures of her in the papers with headlines like 'Love Of Lisa Gives John A Number One!'

In the end the battle at Polydor for what should be the important follow-up, became a straight fight between the Wimps and the Wilds, with John at the head of the Wimps and Willy at the head of the Wilds. Sadly for the future of our star's career, the Wimps won by a small majority.

Even the cover of the single went totally against the previous image of the wild man. A soft focus Otway, with sad eyes, searching a blue lightly clouded sky, graced every copy of that single he felt every punk in the land would be proud to buy.

"I need to do a tour to promote my new single," John told Paul. "But you only finished the last one two weeks ago."

The agency tried their best to explain to John that the sort of tour he had just completed was the sort of thing one did, at the most, once every six months. John did his best to explain that as the last tour had been so incredibly successful, more and more people would come out to see the next one. As usual at this time, John was both wrong and insistent, and so yet another tour of the UK was booked at very short notice.

For this tour, John and Willy had decided to dispense with the services of a band, and go out on tour just as a duo again. On first appearances this should have saved a considerable amount of money, but as Otway now had spending fever, this tour was a financial disaster.

The convoy that toured the country on this tour was a little excessive: Willy took the XJ12 and so John insisted on taking his Bentley, which meant that Potter had to be employed to drive it. He then employed Chris France's girlfriend to polish the car every morning. She would need transport, so Chris drove her to the shows in his car. The gear travelled in the pink van with the two roadies (John and Willy both had their own by this point), Paul Kendall took his Ford Cortina and the P.A. and lights travelled in a three-ton truck.

Everyone on the tour stayed at hotels that Otway felt befitted his and his Bentley's status. Potter clearly remembers one incident that illustrates, probably more than anything else, just how stardom had gone to Otway's head.

"I had just pulled up outside of this hotel, and John insisted that I reverse back three feet as the people in the lobby would not be able to see him getting out of the car from the position I'd stopped in. After getting cross with him about this, I finally relented and backed the car up without looking. I reversed straight into a taxi. Otway was furious at the dent on the back of his car, but the crashing noise did have the effect of attracting the attention of everyone in the lobby, as they noticed both the car and John storming out of it."

'Geneve' did not soar into the charts the way Otway expected it to. In fact it did not soar into the charts at all. About halfway through that tour this fact was pretty obvious. The differences between Otway and Barrett were reaching breaking point.

Willy was still refusing to do Otway's regular seven encores per night and was more than a little miffed at Otway's 'Walt

Disney' record coming out. He had also taken a big interest in gambling and was spending a fortune both in time and money in the bookies. The World Cup was on at this time, and Willy had, by the quarter-finals, got thousands of pounds resting on the results of the matches.

Willy couldn't see the point in doing this tour either. The agent was right about the amount of people that were prepared to come out and see them twice within a month, and Willy had better things to do. Watching the football was one of them.

The last two gigs on the tour were in Penzance then Pontypridd in Wales. They were both very long drives, both bound to lose money, and both coincided with a court case Willy had for the evasion of car tax, and four very important football matches.

When Willy did not show up for those gigs, it was the end of the road for Otway, who had become increasingly sick of Willy's "Lack of professionalism and care over their success."

John sent Willy a telegram saying, "You're fired" and set about approaching the media with his side of the story. 'Willy No Come Back Again' was the headline *Sounds* printed in an issue that had a front cover of Otway diving in the deep end of a hotel swimming pool naked.

John had managed to announce the splitting up of the successful duo on exactly the same day as their new LP 'Deep And Meaningless' was released. "Couldn't you just stay together for a couple of weeks until we have sold some records?" asked the Managing Director of Polydor Records. But Otway was adamant, and John Otway and 'World Cup Willy' were now two individual artistes.

The front cover of that second album probably says it all. There is a picture of Willy with his arms raised heavenwards as if to say "Oh my God! what have I let myself in for?" while Otway just grins with his head resting on Willy's shoulder.

The album did get to number 27 in the LP charts for one week before disappearing without trace.

"How much did we make on the last tour Paul?" John asked. "You lost three grand," was the reply. And so began the years of decline, that Otway was to fight against just as passionately as he had fought for his success in the years before it.

On his own without Willy, John set about finding himself a good band. Tony King, the orchestral arranger of 'Geneve', suggested his son Paul Lilly as a bass player, and he introduced John to a drummer Maurice Bacon.

Maurice had an interesting history, as he had been in several bands and was both the drummer and founder member of the group Love Affair who had had huge hits in the early seventies.

John liked the idea of having stars in his band and so Paul and Maurice formed the nucleus of his new group. Paul Ward from the Otway Barrett band was invited to join on keyboards, and all that was left to find was a guitarist.

John suggested they audition for one, and so a 'Famous Star Wants Guitarist' advert went into *Melody Maker*.

Seventy-five or so guitarists that turned up for the auditions which lasted two days, and it was a difficult job picking someone. "I don't know a good guitarist from a bad one," Otway told his band, "You'll have to pick one. I don't mind making the coffee."

And so, all that Otway's would-be guitarists saw of the star during those auditions was when he walked in to ask, "One sugar or two?"

In the end, everyone was tired and decided on employing the first guitarist they heard. A Scottish chap named Jim Keilt

"One of John's most serious financial errors," says Paul Kendall, "Came in the negotiations of payment for this band. Everyone was quite happy to take a percentage of the profit from both the gigs and the recordings they did, but Otway would have none of it. He thought it was better to pay them a wage, even when they were not working, than give them a slice of the vast fortune that he was sure he was going to make. However, he did not want to be seen as an ungenerous employer, so that band used to get paid a great deal for doing nothing most of the time."

Next, John wanted to go out to the country with his new band, to rehearse. "One needs to get into a creative environment to work", he decided. So the whole band set off to the hills of Snowdonia, to a rehearsal studio next to a hippy commune, to rehearse and to write songs for the next LP.

During his stay down in Wales, John had to rush back for a party he and Kathy had been invited to. The host was Paul McCartney and the party was a reception to launch a new Buddy Holly film.

"It was an amazing evening," John recalls. "Everyone was in high spirits and I'd never seen so many famous people in such a small place. Paul remembered me from the Capital Radio awards thing and introduced me to loads of people, including Keith Moon.

"I liked Keith – we had a couple of things in common. I suppose we were both a bit mad and we both knew Pete Townshend. After the reception, he gave me and Kathy a lift in his limousine to where the film was being shown. I never realised what real fame was until the door of his car was opened and there was just a barrage of camera flashes as he got out.

"He was one of the people I had always wanted to meet. Whenever I mentioned that I'd worked with Pete Townshend, invariably people asked whether I'd met Keith Moon, and it was great knowing that as well as being able to say I had, I also could honestly say he was a good bloke. I mean... I was expecting to walk around to the cinema and he just said 'You can't do that, have a lift'."

After a long expensive period of rehearsal, John was ready to present his new band to the world. There was a pub in London called The Red Cow, which Otway and Barrett had played regularly, and which was one of the places in London that they had a strong pub following. John decided that a full seven nights appearances there would be the ideal way to both introduce the new band and tighten them up for the next tour.

There was a hitch, however. On Thursdays the pub had a drag night when female impersonators rather than bands would take over The Red Cow's stage.

"We can't cancel it," the manager said, "It's been going for years and brings in a hell of a lot of people." "Well, if I do my show in a mini-skirt, could we play all seven nights then?" replied Otway.

And so it was agreed. John could play all the week if, and only if, he was clad in feminine attire for the Thursday night's performance.

"It'll be alright Paul," John told him, "I'll just have to wear a bit of a dress for the first couple of numbers, then I'll have done the drag bit and we can carry on with the normal set."

The first three nights shows went all right, but no press turned up to see the new Otway band. No photographers, no nothing. This was a bit strange. Paul checked with his expensive press agency, Rogers and Cowen. "Yes, they are going to come," he was told. But they hadn't come yet.

So the Thursday night arrived. Kathy had found John an attractive short pink number to wear and, as she had spent several years painting the faces on shop window mannequins, offered to add a little extra in the way of realistic female impersonation by doing his make-up.

The moment he/she stepped on stage that night the reason for the lack of press became obvious. Word had got around. As the 20 or so flashes went off during his first number, John had the first indications that he might have made an error of judgement.

Not much was written about Otway's new band in the reviews that came out of those shows. Quite a bit was written about how ridiculous he looked prancing around doing somersaults in a mini-skirt, and the photos of that performance would haunt him for years. One of these later ended up on the cover of an American LP.

"The dress bit might have launched David Bowie's career," said John later. "But it didn't do a great deal for mine."

John had continued doing his free concerts in Aylesbury, ever since his first one at Bedgrove Pavillion. He liked the title The Annual Otway Free Concert, and the next one coming up would be the first one since the hit. Aylesbury's singing dustman had come a long way in the last 12 months, and Otway wanted to do something really special and really mega as well as really free.

Dave Stopps, being the seasoned promoter in the town, was the obvious man to approach. "What I want to do," John explained to Dave, "is close off the Market Square just like they do on Carnival Day. Only this wouldn't be Carnival Day, it would be Otway Day. The Otway Free Concert to top them all."

Dave Stopps had been talking to Albert Wallace, a documentary director for ATV, and he thought that Otway's preposterous proposal might be the sort of thing in which a major TV company might be interested.

Dave was right. John and Albert met up and Albert was fascinated by this uncoordinated, scruffy, loony who had somehow managed to get a hit and was now planning to close his home town for the day in order to sing it.

So it was agreed, ATV would make a programme, Dave Stopps would promote the concert and Aylesbury would see the biggest Otway Free Concert ever.

Reading festival also wanted John on the bill that year, and so with both a major TV programme and a major festival appearance on the cards, Polydor wanted another single to capitalise on all this publicity.

One of the few up-tempo songs in the Otway repertoire not yet recorded was the old song from his romantic Evesham days, 'Baby's In The Club'. With hindsight, even Otway now accepts that, a) The BBC do not regularly play records about pregnant women, and they were unlikely to make an exception with this song, and b) The most important thing to a punk rocker likely to buy an Otway single was not babies (at least not the type that wear nappies and cry all the time).

Why Otway could not have accepted this with foresight is unknown, but with his usual insistence Polydor were given the job of promoting 'Baby's In The Club' as the next big Otway hit.

For the big Aylesbury gig, John had a huge 12-foot by eight-foot photograph of himself built which looked down on the crowd. The idea was that this could be used as a prop for the forthcoming tour as well. He also wanted to erect signs at Aylesbury railway station which read, 'Welcome to Aylesbury, the home of John Otway" but was informed that he could either have the big photo or the signs but not both. After being told that millions more would see the big photo on TV, he settled for that.

Another Otway idea that was turned down by the authorities was his scheme to be lowered down on to the stage from a helicopter as his band launched into the first chords of the hit.

"I've checked that one out for you," said Albert the director. "The police think it's a little dangerous having a helicopter dangling a few feet above several thousand people. And another thing… it might drown out the music. I think we'll give that one a miss."

The day itself was probably the best day of Otway's life. There had been much concern about the weather, as it had rained each day for the past three weeks. John and Kathy had booked themselves into The Bell Hotel at the bottom of the Market Square the night before.

"I did that for two reasons," John says. "Firstly, The Bell was one of the places I had my first small touches of fame, and that seemed appropriate. Secondly, I wanted to wake up and look out over the Market Square as I got out of bed, to get me in the right sort of mood."

As John got out of bed that morning, he looked out over a sunlit cobbled town centre on one of the sunniest days of that year.

John and Albert went over the songs which Albert wanted to film for the TV. "Apart from 'Really Free', the next most important song is 'Baby's In The Club', John told Albert. "In fact in some ways it is more important because it's going to be the single out at the time."

Albert had a meeting with John's parents, and explained to them that it was important that he knew where they were standing in the audience. He could then, "pan down from their son on the stage, through the audience, and on to them, smiling proudly as their offspring played his hit."

The show went very well. Folks from miles around turned up for John's big day, and gave him the ovation of his life as he took the stage. The whole market square was packed, and John did what he was best at... showing off.

During 'Cheryl's Going Home', traditionally his most wild number, he climbed up the scaffolding like a chimpanzee and did the sort of things reminiscent of his antics on the canal bridge years before. It still looked dangerous and scary, but it was the sort of thing now expected of him, and people thought he knew what he was doing.

John's parents were much better than John at following the advice of the director. They let him know just where they were standing, and there is a lovely shot of just what Albert wanted.

'Baby's In The Club', however, was a disaster. Otway had never played the song live before and got it totally wrong.

What happened was that although Otway started the song off on his own on the guitar, he played the whole first verse in the wrong key. This in itself would not have been quite so bad if Otway had started singing the song in the right key when the band came in. In fact, the whole of the second verse featured John in one key and the band in another. "I always had a bit of a problem pitching my voice," was all he could offer in the way of an explanation later.

More was to come. Straight after the first chorus, the very first thing to be sung in tune, there was a violin solo by John. It is perhaps a shame that John had not informed his roadie Paul Burt about this. Straight after the chorus Otway panicked and can be seen on film lobbing his guitar in the direction of Paul, who was not looking, and tearing around the stage yelling, "Where's my bloody fiddle?"

Aside from this unfortunate incident, Albert Wallace had had some very good footage of a successful concert in the can before the traffic was allowed back into the centre of Aylesbury.

Albert wanted to make the programme with the concert footage interspersed with interviews with both John and the people in the town who had been responsible in some way for his current fame.

John spoke earnestly about how difficult it was having such dedication, knowing that one day he was going to be a star, and about how his ambition was to become so famous that one day he might walk into any pub in Britain and everyone inside would know who he was.

It was Potter's day too. He came on the screen subtitled "Jeff Potter schoolfriend and part-time chauffeur."

He told the story about how, in Primary School, John sent 45 Christmas cards through the school post box to the 45 children in his class, and didn't get one in return. He went on to opine that, "It was destiny that Otway was going to be a huge huge star."

Chris France came on the screen, also subtitled, "Schoolfriend and part-time chauffeur", and related how people would laugh at you if you mentioned you were one of Otway's friends.

Tony Freeth, his old violin teacher, and Tony Redman, his old games and form master, explained just how uncoordinated and scruffy he was at school, and how he seemed to be just the same today.

John's parents were interviewed too. His father told the story of how he mortgaged the house to help with the first LP. His mother said, "I can't really think why he took to singing. I mean, he hasn't got a voice at all. He sings better in tune now than he did, but he can't really sing, can he?"

CHAPTER 22

"I'm not going to go on until you get that photo of me up on that stage where it can be seen," John yelled from his caravan, back-stage at the Reading festival.

It was a week or so after the big Aylesbury concert. The audience, several times the size of the one in John's home town, waited patiently as the roadies dragged the huge picture of Otway from the car park to the stage.

It was a good show, one of Otway's best. There was a mighty cathedral of scaffolding, very high and dangerous, for him to scramble up, and he managed to break six expensive microphones.

"He used to do the same things as Roger Daltrey used to do. You know, swinging the microphone around his head in a big wide circle and then catching it," one of his band recalls. "But with Otway's lack of skill, they used to bounce off peoples' heads or equipment and break. He could never catch them. It was fascinating to watch though. The show seemed to consist of roadies chasing John around the stage and up scaffolding, with new microphones for him to smash up."

As always with Otway, he seemed to polarise the audience. The reviews the following week in the music press reflect this perfectly. *Melody Maker* ran a huge double page on the festival that year with a banner headline reading 'Crazy Otway, Simply Magic', whereas a rival paper in its review just said of his performance, "I suppose there will always be some people who will laugh at stupid things like that."

After festival time, Otway decided it was time to go back on tour to coincide with another record not going up in the charts. For The 'Baby's In The Club' Tour, after the success of his climbing antics, he decided it would be fun to take around two ten-foot scaffolding towers and have a bar between them over the drum kit.

"I'd never done anything like tight-rope walking," explains John, "but I knew it looked pretty impressive. It was a bit dangerous though. I used to hang on to one of the towers and look down. All of the spikes from the top of Maurice's cymbals were pointing menacingly up at me. 'If I fall off, I'm done for' I used to think. I'd just not look down, run as fast as I could along the 12-foot bar and grab the other tower. It must have looked pretty awkward though." "It did," Maurice remembers.

No one quite knows what happened to the 12-foot by eight-foot photograph of Otway. What we do know is that for this tour, Paul Kendall would have had to hire a vehicle twice the size if they had to take the picture with them, and also that the two roadies hated it. It was twice as heavy as any other single item of equipment and three times as awkward. Especially if it had to be carried up three flights of stairs.

On the first day of the tour, John walked on stage asking for it and everyone just shook their heads. "It's bloody strange that we can lose something as big as that, and no one notices that it's missing apart from me," he sulked.

However much research one puts into a book like this, there are a few things that it is impossible to answer. Where the big photograph ended its days is one of them. Another is the number of vehicles that travelled around on that 'Baby's In The Club' Tour. Both the roadies had girlfriends and they had cars. A couple of the band had their own cars, as well as girlfriends, which makes it all a little difficult to work out. Let's just say there was a hell of a lot.

We do know for certain that four vehicles were written off on that tour: one pink van, Paul Kendall's Cortina and two other cars, one of which belonged to the husband of a young lady with whom someone in the entourage was having an affair. How this lady explained to her husband how his car got written off near an Otway gig in Norwich, when she was supposed to be in Oxford, is yet another question that research has been unable to answer satisfactorily.

A chap called Lee Charteris also found his way onto this tour. He was a young and enthusiastic character, who had always fancied being a roadie. He had seen the Aylesbury gig and helped with the equipment on the Birmingham show. He decided to join the tour for the experience. He slept in the truck when no one would put him up on their hotel room floor. The real roadies liked him a lot, because he did all their work for them, and Otway liked him because he treated him like a star.

It was a disastrous tour in many ways though. By the end of it, all of the cash they'd received from Polydor had disappeared.

"We'll have to pull our horns in a little and get an overdraft to tide us over 'till we deliver the next album," Paul Kendall told John. "But you know I want to crack America next, how do you propose we do that on an overdraft?" he replied. "I think America will just have to wait until the next bit of success, don't you?"

John didn't, and for the first time that year, he was worried. Something was going wrong with destiny.

"We had plenty of money at the beginning of the year," he complained, "and it was your job to make sure that we didn't spend it all." "I didn't spend it all, you did," Kendall replied. "But it was your job to make sure I didn't," said Otway angrily.

And they had an argument. It was a pointless argument. Paul Kendall was trying to make Otway see sense and reason, and, as this was something Otway had never done in his life, he saw no point in doing so now. In the end, by mutual argument, they agreed to split up. Otway had the last word, and it was one of his most stupid. "I think I know how to handle money."

For a very short while, John attempted to manage himself. It was not a particularly successful operation. He was no longer greeted in the same way by Polydor, who seemed to be less pleased with the hours that he put in at the offices. More and more often the work-force of each department either had meetings or were out at lunch when Otway called by to find out how they were doing with his records.

Rogers and Cowen set up an interview with the *Daily Mirror* for him. All John could talk to the reporter about was how no one talked to him in the same way since his last two singles had been flops. "Why did you talk about that?" he was asked. "Because it's true," John said.

He went to sort out the money at the bank, only to find he was back in debt again, and it was going to be difficult to get more. "It'll all change when *Stardustman* comes out on TV," John thought. But that came and went.

Although everyone said it was a great and amusing documentary, it did not increase record sales in the way that *The Old Grey Whistle Test* had the year before.

And so John was stumped. "I really didn't know what to do at that point," he admits. "I knew that the next thing I wanted to do was have a go at cracking the States. Everyone told me that they liked English eccentrics over there, and I felt I was one. I told people that it should be easier having hits over there, and more lucrative, but all they used to say was things like, 'Otway, why don't you try and have another hit over here first?' It was a really annoying and frustrating time."

John discussed these problems with Maurice Bacon his drummer, who said that he reckoned he could help sort him out of the mess he was in. "I'll even sort out getting you to America. I saw what was going wrong on that tour, you just need proper sensible management, and you'll be alright."

And so Maurice Bacon became the next person to have a go at managing our star's career. Maurice had worked as Otway's drummer for the last three months and so he did have a certain idea of what he was letting himself in for, but even he was shocked when he took the job on and realised just what a mess everything was in.

The Otway career under the guidance of Maurice Bacon was a lot more sensible and a lot less frivolous, as Maurice had seen his own band, Love Affair, travel to and from the dizzy heights of pop stardom. He was the same age as Otway and Kendall, but in those years he had done and seen a lot more in the music business.

One by one, poor John was stripped of the trappings of success he had so recently acquired.

First to go was the new Otway band. "You can't afford to pay yourself, never mind them," said Maurice. "Look, if it makes you feel better, I'll fire myself first, before I fire the others." And so Maurice left his employment as a drummer.

Next to go were John's press agents, Rogers and Cowen. They had done what Otway had wanted of them over the few months while he was their client. Along with the Paul McCartney party, John had been invited to many other dos, including Shirley Bassey's '25 Years In Showbusiness' bash, where John managed to invite Shirley to his when it came up. There were many others too. People who are regularly seen at these things, doing very little apart from posing and drinking the champagne, are often referred to in the press as 'liggers'. One month Otway did this so regularly that one of the trendier magazines actually made him their 'Ligger of the month'.

Rogers and Cowen had also got John on the TV programme *Star Games*, which featured celebrities from all walks of showbusiness competing in various athletic activities. Otway had done quite well as a member of the Rock Stars team in the obstacle course.

Sadly, as Maurice pointed out, John was now in no position to justify keeping them and they had to go, along with John's position as biggest ligger.

John's Star Car, the Bentley, was put up for sale, and his "old school friends and part-time chauffeurs", became just old school friends again.

"That was the saddest part for me," remembers Chris France. "John only used the car about once a fortnight when he wasn't on tour. If I drove him, then he would let me keep the car the rest of the time. It was the best thing I can ever remember for impressing girls. They used to like getting picked up from home in it, and even their parents used to call me 'The nice boy with the nice car'. After the Bentley was sold I used to pick them up in a car only a little better than the psychedelic A40, and the word 'nice' seemed to get dropped as a description for both me and the car."

John was allowed to keep his big photo cheque book. "But you can only write them out for 'love and kisses' to female fans. If you write them for anything more than that, they'll bounce, and that's not very star-like, is it?" Maurice explained.

About the only tangible thing Otway was able to retain from his many weeks of stardom was his flat. But, as we shall see, even that had to go eventually.

At a small party round at the Otway flat, someone discovered an unopened bottle of champagne in the fridge. As it was passed around, a rather sad voice said, "I was saving that for my next hit," to which someone replied, "Didn't you know? Champagne doesn't last that long."

Maurice banned John from the Polydor offices. "I've been in there to talk to them, and you're driving them mad. I'll concentrate on them, and you concentrate on what you're good at." It would be interesting to know at this point just what Maurice thought John was good at.

After sorting out the financial mess as well as he could, Maurice then attacked the state of John's career. The first and most important thing was records. "You are going to have to do something good recording-wise, before I can even begin to look at America," he said, and went about sorting out some good musicians and a good producer.

The producer both Polydor and Maurice were happy with was Neil Innes. He was the right sort of person to produce John, as he had a flair for humour, having been in The Bonzo Dog Band and having produced the music for *The Rutles* and various other Monty Python spin-off projects. John had no idea, he didn't know what a good producer was any more than he knew what a good musician was. But he and Neil liked each other, and the combination looked as if it could work well.

Between them, Maurice and Neil sorted out the musicians for the next LP and managed to put together a formidable array of talent. The line-up was as follows: Drums – Charlie Morgan, who was at this time in Kate Bush's band. Subsequently he became one of the best session drummers in the country, played on numerous hits, and appeared at Live Aid. Bass – Paul Martinez, another session player, who later joined Robert Plant's band. Keyboards – Morgan Fisher, originally with Love Affair and then Mott The Hoople. He had his own band, Morgan, and after Otway he joined Queen. Guitar – Ollie Halsall, Kevin Ayres' guitarist as well as a session player. The premier American rock magazine, *Rolling Stone*, had his name amongst the 10 top guitarists in the world.

As Otway went into Chappel studios to record the next album, both Polydor and Maurice could be forgiven for thinking that Otway was once more back on track.

Neil Innes did a good job with John, and even the title of the resulting LP, 'Where Did I Go Right', suggests the faith everyone had in this new polished-sounding Otway.

'Frightened And Scared' was one of the "wimp songs played faster" on the LP, and it was picked to be the next single.

John was a man of ideas. Whilst recording that album in the studio, he had been singing along with the backing track of the recording before he had added his voice, when a thought struck him: "I'm more of a live performer than recording artist. Wouldn't it be good if we could sell these records without my voice on? Then I could turn up and stand between the stereo speakers and add both the voice and the performance live, whenever anyone wanted to play it."

Within 10 minutes of thinking this, he realised that it was an impractical idea, but it was original. "And there's not many of those around," he thought. "There must be a way of using it." Eventually he reckoned that not every record should be like that, but maybe a couple of hundred.

Maurice was always good with Otway's mad ideas and schemes, since he appreciated that his success had probably more to do with those than it did with his talent. "You don't need to do a couple of hundred, three is ample," he explained after Otway had told him of this sure-fire way of charting his next single. And he set about organising the 'Live In Your Living Room' promotion.

When 'Frightened And Scared' was released, the cover of every copy of the record bore the message: "If when you play this record you cannot hear John's voice, ring this number and Otway will stand in your living room and add them live!"

As a selling exercise this little gimmick did not work too well. Most of the people who bought John's records had seen him live, and knew only too well the destructive havoc Otway could create on stage – it was the main reason for going to see him. While these people were more than happy to watch this sort of behaviour on stage, and be amused at the clearing-up job he left the roadies with after the show, having Otway do this sort of thing in their own living room was a different matter. It was almost as if John was saying, "Buy my record and I'll destroy your home".

As a promotional exercise it could have been quite good, had it not been for a piece of bad luck. Maurice felt that if he could get some major TV exposure of Otway cavorting around some unfortunate persons front room, the effect on sales could be similar to the *Old Grey Whistle Test* appearance. "ITV news are thinking about doing a piece on it, for the humorous little bit that they put on at the end of the programme," Maurice announced one day.

This was perfect, huge exposure that would have made the whole thing worthwhile. Sadly, ITV rang back: "We'd have loved to have done it," they explained, "But we checked with the Musicians Union, and what John is doing is singing to a pre-recorded track. The M.U. don't allow us to show that on TV so we cannot go ahead with the item."

Of the three possible living rooms that John could have sung in, two of them, or at least their occupants, rang to say that they had upon their turntables a vocal-less record.

The first of these turned up in East Kilbride and Polydor records flew John and an entourage of press and promotions people up to Scotland to do the promised performance.

"It was really odd that," says Otway. "We turned up in this big black limousine to this small house on the outskirts of Glasgow, and this young guy who had bought the record took us in. The front room was full of people from the local papers, the local radio, his family and the five people I'd brought with me. He introduced me to his mum, his grandmother and his sister and her baby. The local paper wanted a shot of me singing to the baby on my knee, so we did that, and then his mum had put on this bit of a buffet so we ate that, and then there were a few more photos and an interview with the radio. It seemed like everyone was putting off the moment when I was to sing.

"I was used to getting up on stage in front of people performing, but the thought of standing in the middle of that living room singing was making me feel really nervous. It seemed to be making everyone else nervous too. They seemed to be looking at me as if to say 'Oh my god, he's going to sing in a minute,' and then thinking of something else to do to delay the performance as long as possible.

"In the end, it couldn't be put off any longer, the record was played and I did the singing bit. I did a couple of somersaults over their settee, and swung on the curtains a bit, but nothing was damaged and they all clapped at the end, probably because the ordeal was finally over."

Another record turned up in the south of London and John and his entourage turned up there to give a similar rendition of the song.

The third record surfaced at a boarding school, where Otway was banned from singing live by the headmaster.

Not enough people purchased themselves a chance to have this sort of personal performance and the record was another flop. There was only one thing for it, John would have to do yet another tour to promote the new LP.

No Bentley, chauffeurs or polishers accompanied this tour. More importantly though, the whole band apart from the drummer agreed to go out on the road with John to promote the new record.

It was a good tour and it even made money. John did not like travelling in the minibus, but he did appreciate the fact that he could pay the rent after the tour was over. The band was the tightest and most professional ever.

The first show was at The Venue in Victoria, London, an old converted cinema with a very high arch above the stage. Recalling his wish to be lowered onto the stage by helicopter while the band played the opening chords of the hit, John found a long rope and decided to lower himself the 50 or so feet to the stage as a form of grand entrance. "Great idea," said Paul Martinez, the bass player. "And Ollie and I can jump down from this scaffolding at the same time."

It sounded like a great idea and so they rehearsed it. Otway was fine. He came tearing down the rope, and only removed the top layer of skin from his hands in the process. Ollie took one look at the jump from the scaffolding, and decided to leave the acrobatics to John and Paul. Paul leapt perfectly on time and hit the ground at the same time as Otway, perfectly on cue for the first lines of the song. Unfortunately he also broke his leg.

"That looks great," said Maurice to Paul who was writhing on the floor. "I think we can go with that."

They couldn't go with that. Paul did that concert, and most of the subsequent shows, seated, his leg in a plaster raised up on a chair.

However good this show was, and it was good, it did more for Otway as a loony stage performer than it did as a recording artist. The new LP did not even venture near the album charts and by the end of that tour Otway was ready for his next major career move.

"Now can we go to the States?" he asked.

CHAPTER 24

Otway now looked on America as the way destiny had in mind for him to achieve international stardom, and Britain was merely the place where he had served his apprenticeship. Maurice was sent on a reconnaissance mission to New York, to prepare the continent for the forthcoming invasion.

In many ways it was a good time to try this venture. The Americans were just beginning to show an interest in the new wave music coming out of Britain, and Freddy Laker had drastically cut the cost of travelling the Atlantic. Dire Straits, an English pub band, had just become huge stars over there, and bands like The Police and Squeeze looked like doing the same thing.

Luckily, John's booking agency were the English agents for The Police, and through them Maurice met Ian Copeland, their American agent. He was interested enough to offer to get John a few dates should he decide to come over. He was also able to sort out the correct visas and work permits.

On his short mission, Maurice had done well and came back with the exciting news that a short but extensive tour of America had been pencilled in. This tour would cover both the East and West coasts, a couple of dates in the Mid-West and two dates in Canada.

Unlike Otway, Polydor did not see America as the place where they were likely to recoup the huge losses they had already made on him and his records. "Releasing records in America is an expensive business," they said. "There has been no demand for John's records on import in the States, and so we see no reason to incur further losses on either supporting a tour or issuing product in that territory."

"But once we do a few dates and they realise that I'm big

news over there, they won't be able to get records out quick enough," John told Maurice.

Although Maurice could usually control John's spending, there were times when he was adamant and stubborn. If it meant getting back on the treadmill of debts and overdrafts in order to achieve some goal, then so be it. His motto was: "If I have to borrow thousands of pounds in order to make it in America, then these can easily be paid back from the mountain of dollars I will earn."

And so Maurice was pushed into sorting out this tour. All he could do, faced with this determination, was to do it as cheaply as possible, and keep borrowing down to a minimum.

"John was very excited about the prospects of going to America," Jeff Potter remembers. "He would run around the front room of his flat, making airplane noises, followed by a yell of 'Hello America'."

For obvious monetary reasons, Otway was back working as a duo again in the US. This time with Ollie Halsall on guitar.

John and Ollie did a few shows to warm up this line-up, including a couple at John's old haunt, The Oranges And Lemons in Oxford. They also did an extraordinary thing, they got together and wrote some songs.

For a while it was a very productive partnership, and in the short period of time between the last tour and going to the States, John and Ollie wrote a lot of material, including 'Cry Cry', '21 Days', 'Body Talk', 'When Love's in Bloom' and 'Day After Day'.

'Cry Cry' was yet another song about the suffering that our hero went through as a struggling sensitive artist:

Pain and sorrow and sadness and tears,
I've been suffering all these years.
Staying alive is killing me.
With heartache, sickness and misery,
Doom, disaster and tragedy.

This gives some idea of what it felt like having to wait for another hit.

'Day After Day', however, is a lovely song, one of those rare occasions when John could write sensitively about his deeply personal feelings:

They say that it's colder in Northern Alaska,
And that it's hotter down by the Equator.
I've had these hot and cold feelings in my bones,
Day after Day.
Waking up, the same situation the same things to say.
The same conversations I had

As I started chasing
You kept on running away.

"It was one of the few things I ever wrote that people would always harp on about, and ask why I didn't write more things like that."

The Otway entourage consisted of John, Kathy, Ollie and John Rummens, a friend of Kathy's from art school days. Otway liked him: he was diplomatic, charming and had the ability to talk his way out of awkward situations. He had lived in Texas for a number of years while on a post-graduate course, and had some idea of what Americans were like. He was just the sort of person Otway needed to smooth the way through the ultra-low budget tour planned for him. He was hired as tour manager.

Maurice flew out a few days early to organise what press and promotion he could and was due to meet them in New York. Cheap Atlantic flights in those Laker days were strange affairs, as a price-cutting war was going on between the companies. Maurice had worked out the cheapest possible way to take advantage of this war and had given Rummens the job of putting this into effect. It was very un-starlike.

Basically, it entailed phoning all the major airlines to find out if there were likely to be any stand-by seats available, and if there were, queueing at the airline office from about four in the morning. If you were lucky, you would get seats for that day's flights.

A lot of people were taking advantage of these new cheap flights, and the queues were always long. However, few of these people were about to embark on a tour – with amplifiers, guitars, flight cases of equipment, records and merchandising as well as luggage. Imagine the horror of the poor girls on the stand-by desks, used to passengers with one suitcase and ready to travel immediately, watching the four trolley loads of rock and roll gear edging slowly but inexorably towards them.

"There seemed to be a lot of: 'How many tickets did you need? Four? What a shame we just have three for this last flight'," John remembers.

Rummens learned the trick that free LPs and tee-shirts could smooth the way through a lot of travel problems. "You might not have heard of John Otway, but your daughter will have. Do you want John to sign an album for her?" he would say, and it would ease the situation considerably.

Even with this smoothing, it still took four days of getting up at four am and getting disappointed after eight hours of queueing before the star took off from Heathrow and headed for Washington D.C.

"But isn't Maurice going to be meeting us in New York?" John asked. "Shut up," said Rummens.

Maurice was indeed supposed to meet them in New York. He had even organised some American girls with banners to greet them at Kennedy airport.

Even though Washington was several hundred miles from both New York and the welcoming party, and no transport had been organised between the two, Otway was happy. Washington was the first place where Otway genuinely raised his arms in the air in the manner he had rehearsed so often in his flat and yelled. "Hello America".

In the arrivals lounge of Washington International Airport, Ollie was not amused. He was a guitarist of considerable status, who had in the past done several proper American tours. He was used to going to the right airport, and being met by a representative of the record company, who would then organise his transport to his hotel where he could recover from his jet-lag. He was not used to being asked if he could "keep an eye on the gear for an hour or so while we go and see if we can get a car."

Rummens eventually hired a station wagon that could carry themselves and the equipment, as long as John and Ollie sat with their guitars on their knees. The four rather cramped travellers set off on the long journey to Manhattan. In fact the conditions were so cramped, and they were all so tired, that they ended up splitting the ride and spent the first night in Philadelphia, before meeting up with Maurice the following day.

It is true that a lot of Americans love England. They like its culture, its history, its music and its eccentrics. John was amazed at how easily he was accepted by the citizens of New York. On their first night in that city, they all went down to a club called Hurrahs, which they would be playing in a few days time.

"Some people had actually heard of me," John says. "Hurrahs was bringing over a lot of the new English acts, and a lot of the audience read the English music papers. After going to that club I really thought that cracking the Big Apple was going to be a piece of cake."

The first American venue to host an Otway show was The Paradise Club in Boston. John and Ollie were supporting Iggy Pop. It was quite a good bill as both acts were pretty wild, and the turnout was good. It was also a strong start to that tour and the duo went down well enough to get an encore.

"Now we've got Boston under our belts, let's get New York," Otway said on the long drive back.

They were headlining at Hurrahs, the advance publicity had been organised well, and Otway was nervous enough to put on a pretty wild show.

A lot of people turned out to see Ollie. Both Patto and Kevin Ayres, whom Ollie had worked with, had something of a cult following, and anyone who was into guitarists knew his name. These people were different from those who normally came to see Otway, as they had a taste for music rather than extravagance. They all liked the show. It was something new to the Americans, who would say things like, "Hey this guy is really crazy."

After the second encore that night, Otway was convinced that if he could "make it there he could make it anywhere". Already, after the first few days of that tour, two major cities had fallen to the small invasion force.

The invasion force was to get smaller too. On the way to Philadelphia, Maurice mentioned in passing, that money could be saved on hotel rooms if John and Kathy shared a twin room with Ollie. That was enough for Kathy who was, at this point, crammed in the back with John, Maurice and the guitars. She took the Greyhound bus down to Texas, and spent the duration of that tour with some of Rummens' friends in El Paso.

After a few more days on the East Coast, it was up north across the border and into Canada to play Toronto. The Edge Club there, was one of those places ideally suited to the sort of show John and Ollie were doing – both in size and atmosphere. Oddly enough, more people here had heard of Otway than anywhere else. There was even a group of émigrés from Aylesbury who turned up to cheer him on. Toronto was to witness John's greatest successes in North America. They played several nights and the audience grew with each subsequent performance.

The longer distances could be flown as cheaply as driven by the trio left on the tour. Having played Detroit and Chicago, they flew the long journey to the West Coast and Vancouver.

The dates on the West Coast were supporting the American band Pere Ubu. "We really did well in Vancouver," Otway remembers. "The show started brilliantly because I tripped and fell flat on my face as I walked on stage. The audience liked that, and from that point on, I couldn't seem to do any wrong.

"Pere Ubu seemed a little miffed, and the atmosphere was a bit strained in the dressing room in San Francisco a couple of nights later. It didn't help that we'd flown down and they'd had a two day drive in a van. It all changed though. The first set that night was hell. Pere Ubu seemed to be pretty big news in San Francisco, and the Frisco crowd appeared to want to get us off stage as quickly as possible. After about the third number, they started yelling things like, 'Get off', and 'Quit using the phoney English accents'.

"Well, heckling like that always made me go a bit wilder, and in this case, it made the audience go a bit wilder too. The place was selling food, and there were all these sachets of tomato ketchup on the tables. The audience discovered that these made really good missiles, and that a carefully aimed sachet would explode on impact.

"Pere Ubu's lot couldn't believe it as we arrived back in the dressing room during the break. On first sight it looked as though a mad knife man had been hacking away at us for the whole of that first set.

"Anyway, we cleaned ourselves up, and put on clean shirts for the second set. The trouble was, as soon as we walked on stage to do it, someone yelled 'Oh no, it's them again!' and another load of ketchup came flying through the air. So we were back looking like mad knife man victims again before we'd even plugged in our guitars.

"After that Pere Ubu were really nice to us. They even came out to watch some of that show."

It is widely believed that people on the West Coast of America are more 'laid-back' than those on the East. If this is true, then it seems that laid-back Americans do not like crazy ungainly loonies. Ollie, whose playing was universally liked, impressed them, but John's mad antics did not go down so well.

For example, whilst Ollie was playing a long solo, his head and body bopping around as he entertained these people with his brilliant playing, John would sneak up behind him and pull his guitar lead from his amplifier.

People who admired Otway's very odd sense of humour, found it hilarious to see Ollie, mid-bop and mid-riff suddenly silent, with John standing behind him grinning holding up a jack-plug.

People like Ollie, people who admired good playing, and laid-back Americans found it horrible.

Otway jokes like, "This is a song about the American Civil War, it's called 'Remember The Alamo'," and his impersonation of Sammy Davies Jnr. consisting of John singing 'I see trees of green, red roses too,' in a low gravelly voice, were taken by these audiences, probably correctly, as a lack of brain cells rather than comic genius.

The effect of the invasion force on the West Coast of America was probably summed up brilliantly by Otway, who said wryly after one gig: "When I wrote the lines 'And my dreams, will see me playing for the screaming ladies of Los Angeles', I wasn't dreaming of them screaming 'Get off!'"

The Otway newsletter, written from that part of the States to his fans back home, tells a much different story. A story about how everybody "Just loves me over here," and the inevitable "It really looks as though I'm going to be an international star now."

"Well I wanted my 'Letter from America', to be optimistic," says John now. "And apart from those dates on the West Coast, I did feel we had almost made it there."

John and Ollie played a couple more shows in New York on the way home. It was a good way to end that first trip. They had indeed built a small reputation. Ian Copeland came and saw one of the shows and was impressed enough to sign Otway to his agency. By the time Otway got on that plane home he was happy and confident. There were now two places in that huge continent where Otway could genuinely claim that he had the embryo of a cult following.

The problem was yet again Otway's faith in his ultimate destiny. He believed that as long as one went down well somewhere, the next time one played, the audience would double, and then keep doubling until the figures were so huge, that they did indeed amount to massive fame.

This sort of chain-letter, or rather chain-audience, theory was obviously flawed, but his successes, especially in Toronto and New York, were, he felt, strong enough reasons to attempt to put this theory into practice.

CHAPTER
25

Back in England John was bored. He had enjoyed the electricity of America. Over here Polydor had not missed him and, however often they were told just how many records they could sell in the States, they were adamant about not putting out John's records over there.

"Well if they won't, someone else will," John insisted, and gave Maurice the job of buying back the rights to North America from Polydor. Polydor were delighted at the idea of getting something back from Otway, and at last felt that his tour had been worth it.

It was easily done. John's commitment to Polydor was reduced from four LPs to three. Which meant that after just one more album they could be free of one of their biggest loss-making artists.

On his return to England, John spent a considerable amount of time in the studio with Ollie in an attempt to record some of the songs they had written and worked out together. The tour they had just completed had taken its toll on the relationship though: the recordings amounted to nothing and the two of them went their separate ways.

Having the rights to get his records released in America, John's main interest lay on the other side of the Atlantic and getting a record company and hits over there. As soon as Maurice could be persuaded, John was back over on the East Coast again, but this time with a band.

"After doing so well with Ollie I thought this'll really do it. The Americans like bands, especially English ones," says John. "I knew it was going to be expensive taking a band over, but in order to maintain the momentum of my career, I really needed to get America in the bag."

The band he took over for this second tour was badly under-rehearsed. One short day of practice is not really enough time for a band that has the job of taking America by storm, especially as the guitarist had never heard any of the songs before. But one short day of rehearsal was all they had.

"If John wanted me to get him an American record deal," complained Maurice, "he could at least have taught his band the songs."

Having a band necessitated having a roadie. "But it will have to be someone very cheap," said Maurice. "Well what about that guy who used to sleep in the back of the van on the last British tour, I bet he'd do a tour of America for nothing," replied Otway, and he was right, he did.

Lee Charteris was a very enthusiastic, ambitious and smart chap, who happened at the time to look on Otway as a bit of a hero. As Lee left for America, he felt that his big break had come. Fate moves in mysterious ways, and strangely enough for Lee Charteris working with Otway was the start of a long and prosperous career.

John found that having someone like Lee opened up whole new areas of theatrical entertainment, and from this point on the abuse of roadies would become one of the focal points of the Otway show.

It started off simply enough, with John tossing the guitar to Lee when he didn't need it. With Otway's coordination though, what for most people would have been a simple toss and catch became something quite different as Lee vividly remembers.

"You could see by where John was looking, and the motion of his arms and body, which direction he was intending to throw the guitar. But the intended direction of this musical projectile, and the direction it actually took had nothing in common at all."

This meant that Lee had a similar task to that of a goalkeeper facing a penalty kick on Cup Final day. When Lee 'saved' a guitar, the response from the crowd was also similar.

Otway instantly spotted that response. Before long, Lee had got good at saving those tosses, so the tosses became hurls to the side of the stage. As soon as Lee had got used to saving these hurls, Otway changed the times when he hurled.

"Suddenly, for no reason at all, he'd just take off his guitar and chuck it, without even looking," says Lee. For the whole of the one-hour show, Lee would stand at the side of the stage poised and ready to catch John's instruments.

"There were problems," recalls Lee wryly. "The worst was when John stood on his guitar lead when he was throwing. Normally, by the time the guitar had left his hands, John had no further control on its direction, so you had some idea of which way the instrument was going, and how you were going to catch it. If he was standing on the lead though, you never knew when the lead was going to run out, which would stop the guitar's normal trajectory and send it plummeting vertically to the stage. We lost quite a few guitars like that."

The combination of Lee's athletic abilities and the way Otway made his job unreasonably difficult was a definite crowd pleaser. "You could always rely on Lee to win audience sympathy," says John. "Girls would come up to him afterwards and put their arms around him saying 'How can you let that stupid man treat you like that?' But Lee used to love it."

This new piece of theatre did to some extent make up for the lack of musical experience, but it was not the right way to get a record deal. Depression set in amongst the band to such an extent that on the way home, the guitarist consumed his whole bottle of duty-free gin on the plane, and staggered away from Heathrow Airport saying "Never again." Otway hasn't seen him since.

The loss of this guitarist was a little catastrophic, since two days after the band's arrival home, Maurice had organised a tour of Scandinavia, Ireland and the UK. Swedish television had just shown John's documentary, *Stardustman*, and Polydor in Sweden had just released the LP and single to capitalise on this exposure. It was one of the best opportunities Otway would have to export his talent to other lands.

The bass player, Alan Offer, was a quiet easy-going chap, with a dry sense of humour that stretched as far as finding Otway amusing. He bought in George Lloyd, the guitarist from his last band, and took it upon himself to make sure that the new line-up sounded better than the old one did on the first gig. It did.

But everyone in Scandinavia, Ireland and the UK were asking the same question. It was a question Otway was even asking himself. When was he going to have another hit?

It was time to record again. Polydor were encouraging Otway to give them the last LP so that they could complete their part of the contract as soon as possible, and anyone Maurice spoke to regarding an American deal wanted to hear some new material.

Otway was stumped. The last LP had not made any impact, and John started finding its title, 'Where Did I Go Right', embarrassing.

"If I can't make it with a hundred piece orchestra or a proper band and producer, what do I do?" Otway asked, fearing the inevitable, "Well it worked with Willy."

What had Mr. Barrett been up to during this time? Well...

After he and John split up, he recorded his own solo album, 'The Call Of The Wild'. The sleeve showed Willy holding up a card with Otway on it as the Joker, and the single from this LP was an instrumental track entitled, 'I Did It Otway'.

Willy discovered two acoustic guitars of John's in the back of the XJ12. He thought it would be amusing to record himself playing a bit of rag-time music and sawing John's instrument up at the same time. He could then send the tape to John, with a note saying, "Sorry, I didn't realise it was your guitar 'till I'd finished recording the track." In the end, he felt it was even funnier to get a photograph of him sawing the other guitar. "I just thought the tape and photograph together would have the greatest impact on Otway," he said. And he was quite right.

When Otway opened his mail one morning, he was heard to yell, "That's my bloody guitar," as he looked at the photo. "That's my other bloody guitar," he yelled as he heard the tape.

Willy reacted to getting money from Polydor in a totally different manner to John. He had used the record company's money to build his own studio, where he could record his album and saw up John's guitars. But neither Otway nor Barrett had had any record success during their separation, and financial necessities made some sort of reconciliation a wise course of action. "I'm sure that we both hated the idea of getting back together, but we were both greedy," says John.

Greed is a very creative energy source in the hands of the desperate, and within a short time there was enough material to make up the next LP.

Recording at Willy's home-made studio did have its problems. The wiring was chaotic and the fridge downstairs made a big clicking noise on the tape every time it cut in.

They did do some interesting things, like speeding the tape up halfway through a song, when Willy felt it needed a key change. Even though it was done at the expense of making Otway's voice sound suddenly squeaky.

The most interesting track on the LP was undoubtedly 'DK 50/80'. Willy had produced a track called 'KD 80/50' for Ken Liversausage years ago, and whilst checking through some tapes had accidentally played it backwards. The chorus sounded interesting like that, so John sang some forward verses over a drum machine pattern and the pair put together what could possibly be described as a prototype scratch record.

The title of the LP came from the design for the cover, with the names Otway and Barrett spread over the front and back, with only the 'Way and Bar' on the front.

The first single off this LP was 'Birthday Boy', a quirky little number, with the almost catchy chorus line, 'Who's a lucky birthday boy, everybody's going to sing.'

The album came out, and the single came out, and the reformed duo were not heading towards the hit parade. "There's no way round it," Otway said., "We're going to have to hype the charts."

Otway's attempts at hyping the charts show our hero at his most inventive and his most desperate.

He now needed success more than ever. He had run out of money, there was no more due from Polydor, and no other record company, over here or over there, was likely to be interested in giving him a contract after such a consistent series of failures. He was determined to get another hit at all costs, even if it meant cheating.

Cheating has been around almost as long as the charts themselves, and almost everyone does it. Some attempts at artificially making hits are simple in the extreme: drive around the country buying lots and lots of records from the right shops. These attempts often fail. Otway didn't feel like spending a few weeks buying his own records, which he could not afford, and then getting an expose in the Sunday Papers with pictures of himself wheeling a trolley-load of his records out of a record shop. "I often did buy my own records," admits John, "But that's hardly the thing I wanted to be famous for."

He knew that somehow enough people had to be persuaded to buy the next single from the right shops in large enough quantities. "We could send out a hundred record tokens to everyone on the newsletter list," he suggested to Maurice, who replied with the exact sum that they would need to borrow to do that. A quick call to the bank manager and a few friends made that idea out of the question.

"Lots of people come to my shows to see me live," Otway thought. "They just don't buy my records. Is there a way of making them?" And then it occurred to him. There was.

The average price of a ticket to see a gig at that time was about £2.00 and the average price of a record was £1.25. So he decided to do a tour, with the stipulation that anyone could get in to see it free if they have a copy of the next single, and if they haven't got a copy, then they can't get in at all.

"If I tear round the country and play enough towns that have the right record shops in them, then I'm going to sell enough ticket/records to get me a hit."

It was an original idea, something no one had done before. The reasons no one had done this before were, in fact, quite obvious, as Maurice pointed out: a) Otway and Barrett would be doing the whole tour for nothing and would earn not a penny; b) There would be no money to pay for accommodation, petrol, or for anyone else on the tour; c) Willy did not want to do it unless they took a band; d) The places played in would earn no money for staging the concerts; e) Any money from record sales would be swallowed up by Polydor, to pay back the massive advance; f) The agency that booked the gigs for Otway took 15 per cent commission, which on this tour would amount to precisely £0.00 They also needed to find a complete and up-to-date list of where the chart return shops were.

The list of chart shops was easy, as Otway discovered – almost everyone in the music industry had some sort of accurate list. The other parts however were not so easy, and Maurice set about solving them one by one.

It was Maurice that came up with the idea of campsites. "They are a lot cheaper than hotels," he explained. "For a fiver a night, you can put a tent up in a campsite, and I can get you a tent that'll hold the whole band."

"That's great for my star image," muttered Otway. "But, John look at this," said Maurice, showing Otway the *A.A. Book Of Campsites*. "Some of these places are four star campsites. You've never been able to afford four star hotels, have you?"

Otway agreed to do the tour as long as they stayed at no campsite that was lower than two star.

The tack Maurice used with the agency, the band and the roadie were essentially the same: help us out with this and we'll have a hit – in the end you'll all do really well out of it.

The only person this tack did not work on was Lee the roadie. "They must be bloody joking. Not only am I supposed to do another tour for nothing for them, I'm also expected to play Boy Scout as well."

As it happened, Roadie Lee's 'performances' on stage had not gone unnoticed. Toby Errington, one of the locals at the Warrington, had seen him in action, and was so impressed with his ability to keep Otway's show going, that he got him a job as roadie for the band Queen. This not only gave Lee a very decent wage, but also the four star hotels that John could not afford. And Lee has been considerably richer than John ever since.

The agency had no easy task to earn their 15 per cent of nothing. They had to find dates in specific cities over a three-week period. It is lucky that many pubs do not expect to make money on the door for the entertainment they provide, and are quite happy selling the extra drink to a larger clientele. It is these places that John's agents, Wasted Talent, approached.

"A lot of people worked really hard to get that tour off the ground," says John. "Bob Gold from the agency did an almost impossible job booking those dates. John Pearson at Polydor worked like a mole in the company for us 'cause he really liked the idea. Without him enough records would not have got in the shops, and the idea would not have worked at all."

On June 23 1980, two vans, one with all the equipment associated with a rock and roll tour and one with all the equipment associated with a camping holiday, set off on The Tent Tour – a grand Otwayesque venture to make 'DK 50/80' a hit. One of these vans headed straight for the venue to set up for the night's show, and the other headed straight for the campsite to set up for the night's sleep.

It was obvious from the first night that to some extent the plan was working. John had kept his live following remarkably intact over this period of record failure, and about two hundred punters turned up with records for that first show.

John Rummens came both to tour manage and to check the records on the door. "You could tell what people thought of Otway records though," he says. "Loads of them turned up with their records folded up in their pockets."

The new Otway Barrett show was good. Spurred on by the possibility of another hit, the pair were in fine form, and differences, for a while, forgotten.

Camping was fun too. Willy had bought a game of swingball to pass the leisurely hours on the campsite. As it was Willy's swingball he soon became tour champ. Otway as can be imagined was tour loser.

"I had bruises on my fingers for a lot of that tour, from getting too close to the Wild Willy serve," remembers John.

Issy Brampton, Chris France's old girlfriend, (the one who used to polish Otway's Bentley on more extravagant tours) came along to sell programmes and T-shirts. It was hoped, and it worked out, that merchandising income would pay for the campsites and petrol.

The second and third nights were equally successful as the first, and as The Tent Tour made its way up the country on its first leg, the campers were beside themselves with excitement and anticipation to see what the chart position would be when it came out on the Tuesday morning.

Tuesday morning arrived, and Rummens was kicked out of his sleeping bag and sent off to get the news as well as the milk that morning.

Yes! It was working! 'DK 50/80' had indeed broken into the Top 75. Otway was cheating, and cheating well. "It's another hit record," he beamed. "Now lets make this one a number one." What's more, *Top Of The Pops* had asked about John's availability, should the record go up the following week.

There was a hitch though. The BBC were in dispute with the Musicians Union, and there was a strong possibility that there would be no *Top Of The Pops* the next week.

After another week of camping the record had gone up again. All these people coming to see the Otway and Barrett show had now pushed the record up to 45 in the charts.

"We're on our way," said Otway. But no *Top Of The Pops*. "Bloody Musicians Union, that's another hit they might've stopped me having," he said with a little justification.

They did get one TV appearance out of it – a Saturday morning ITV show called *Fun Factory*. As usual, given a good opportunity, John and Willy could be guaranteed to do something ridiculously stupid.

They were both fans of the TV show *Tiswas*. This series had just finished and *Fun Factory* had taken its Saturday morning spot. The show was filmed live, and John and Willy were woken early in the tent that morning to travel to Granada Studios in Manchester.

"As it's going out live," John said to Willy, "We can do something shocking." Willy wrote "TISWAS" in huge letters on the back of his guitar, and during the guitar solo, when his instrument filled millions of screens up and down the country, Wild Willy flipped his guitar over and advertised *Fun Factory*'s rival programme.

This jolly jape did not go down a bomb with the TV company, who felt it was not the nicest way for the duo to thank them for giving them a bit of a break. It didn't help sales either. The Tent Tour had only a week to go and, as the only people buying these records appeared to be those who wished to go to the shows, sales started falling.

As the two vans hit Scotland, they got the news that the record had just gone down to 47. It was a good try. Maybe if people had started to buy the record because they liked it and wanted a copy of it, its small success might have been the start of a bigger hit. Had they done *Top Of The Pops*? Who knows.

Otway for a while would claim that he had in fact had two hits, and the *Guinness Book Of Hit Records* does have both. But it was such a source of humour – whenever he was asked how high the other hit got – that John accepted that he was still, at that point, just a one hit wonder.

CHAPTER 27

So it was time to say goodbye to Polydor. John remembered reading that in the last financial year Polydor had lost eight million pounds and, since he felt responsible for a bit of it, wondered what he could do to help.

"Why don't we do a benefit concert for them?" John asked Maurice. "I mean, they helped us out and got me a hit record, it would be nice to do something for them."

Surprisingly, everyone apart from Polydor themselves agreed that it would be nice, and The Venue in Victoria was chosen as the place to stage this event. "Funny that," says John. "The Venue was owned by Virgin Records and they were quite happy to stage a benefit for a rival company."

In fact lots of other record companies helped out. Maurice got many of them to donate records to raffle off on the night. Stiff records had a house band (a group whose members were Stiff employees) called the Stiff All Stars. They said they would love to donate an evening's performance in aid of another company who had lost so much money.

Polydor's greatest success over the past couple of years had been with the Bee Gees, after *Saturday Night Fever*. At this time, a band called the Hee Bee Gee Bees had a hit, 'Meaningless Songs In Very High Voices', which owed much to The Bee Gees phenomenon. They had much to thank Polydor for too, and they would help out.

As mentioned before, the chaps on the executive floor of the Polydor building did not seem as enthusiastic about this magnanimous gesture as everyone else. Even though the Managing Director of the corporation was invited to the event, and was promised The Venue's equivalent of the Royal Box, the kind offer was politely declined.

On the lower floors of the building, where no one seemed as concerned about "head office in Hamburg finding out", the response was much more encouraging. Many a Polydor minion took the offer of a free ticket to the concert in aid of their company, and the two tables at the front of the stage were reserved for them.

After The Tent Tour, Willy's latest Racing Car Guitar, the biggest, fastest and ugliest version of the instrument so far, had been left at the Polydor Offices – in fact in the office of one Dennis Munday.

"Otway," Dennis moaned, "when are you going to remove that damn instrument from my office? I keep tripping over it, which is painful as there's sharp bits of angle iron sticking out of its chassis. It's been there a month and you're not even on Polydor any more." "Er... um... well we're going to raffle it off at the benefit," Otway said quickly.

Two days before the event, John was told that four employees had got together and formed a Polydor house band, especially for the concert, and were calling themselves Polly Door And The Benny Fits.

On the night of the concert The Venue was packed. There was a large cardboard thermometer on the stage with 'POLYTHON' in large letters underneath. The red bit in the middle of this thermometer rose through the evening as money was donated to the company. Otway and Barrett walked on stage to thank everyone for coming in support of such a good cause and introduced the first band.

The two Polydor tables were packed. "Wow," said John. "More Polydor people have turned up tonight than ever did when we were with the company."

Those seated at those tables were well looked after. As well as free admission, they were given free raffle tickets and some free wine. The audience applauded wildly as Willy pointed to them from the stage and said: "These people at these tables here are the reason we have all gathered here tonight."

One of the evening's highlights was the auction. "I have here," said Willy, "a box of 25 records kindly donated by CBS. They are the song that came third in the battle for the UK entry for the Eurovision song contest. Do I hear 50 pence?" With these and similar donated records, £10 was added to the Polython.

One of the surprises of the raffle was that it was won by Dennis Munday from Polydor, who did very well with his free ticket and won the Racing Car Guitar. "Mr Munday can pick his prize up from his own office on Monday morning," announced Willy.

By the end of the night, the red bit in the middle of the thermometer had risen to £1,300.

A week or so later, at a Polydor conference, Otway and Barrett arrived with a violin case stuffed with £1,300 one pound notes, and presented it to Tony Morris the Managing Director.

It would appear that head office in Hamburg had not got to hear of the benefit concert. On receiving the money he gave a speech. "I would like to thank Messrs Otway and Barrett," he said, "and I would like to see more and more of our acts donating the money they get from their live performances to us." Whether he meant this or not, no one knows, as no other act has ever done anything similar since.

Having another 'hit', even one that only got as far as 45, did have some advantages, one of them being that mild attention was paid to them by other record companies. After short negotiations, this attention was quickly reduced to one record company, Stiff Records.

Stiff was a company whose success had largely been built on getting hit records for oddballs. They were also expanding into the American market and starting a Stiff America label. "Perfect," said Otway. "Perfect," agreed Maurice. And Stiff were happy too.

So Otway had got essentially what he felt he needed, an American deal. "So we can now go and crack America properly," Otway said to Barrett. "Sod off," said Barrett. "You lost a fortune trying to do that last year, I'm not going."

"Willy is not interested in international stardom," John complained to Maurice, and after a lot more arguments, John and Willy split up yet again. And John prepared for his first mega-tour of the States.

John would spend six of the next 12 months in the States, trying more and more desperately and more and more expensively to get the continent under his belt.

During this period, John and Willy would get together and split up a further three times. John would hardly ever be home during this year of touring, and by the end of it, he and Kathy would have drifted apart and split up.

The American tours were incredibly tough, with thousands of miles covered by the Otway band in a van. "They had a heatwave over there," says John, "in which a lot of people died. That was the summer we had to cross the Arizona desert twice in a wretched van with no air conditioning."

Otway's chain-audience theory was also eventually disproved over this period. As Mark Freeman his drummer vividly recalls. "Yeah, we'd get in this van, drive all day for 13 hours, spend the night in a cheap motel, travel to the show for the following night for another eight hours, and then play to 50 people in some mid-western city. 'Wow that went down a storm,' John would say. 'Next time we go the place'll be packed.' And so we'd do the whole trip again and go down a storm to the same 50 people."

It was a bit easier with Stiff putting out records over there, but not a lot. Stiff had just started their American operation. Their methods of promoting and marketing, which worked so well in the UK, did not work as well in the USA. They did do a repeat of the 'Live in your apartment' promotion, and John managed to get onto the *Six O'Clock News* in New York, singing in someone's front room.

They were miles away from real fame though, and Otway's time over there was spent getting only a splattering of fans dotted around that continent.

After 10 weeks of this, the Otway band returned tired and poorer, and Steve Bolton, John's guitarist for the tour, left and joined Paul Young's band.

On a day off in Minneapolis, Otway had booked a studio and recorded a live version of 'Green Green Grass Of Home', that had been going down so well in the shows. Stiff liked the recording, as it captured the lunacy of the Otway show without sounding too bad, and released it.

For the cover of this single, Stiff took the Tom Jones cover, crossed out his name and replaced it with 'John Otway'. Similarly, they stuck John's face over the top of Tom's, so that a grinning Otway head was perched on top of the Jones' body.

Times had changed. The old punk music had developed and was now known as New Wave. This was simply because bands that had succeeded because they played badly had improved. Otway had succeeded because he played badly, but hadn't improved at all. And as we all know, 'Green Green Grass Of Home' was not the sort of hit for John as it had been for Tom.

Maurice got John together with Chris Burkett, a friend of his, who had been in Love Affair. As well as being a pretty neat guitarist, he worked as an engineer in a studio. He was a talented chap and he and Otway got together and wrote Otway's next batch of songs, including 'Middle Of Winter', 'Too Much Air Not Enough Oxygen' and 'Turning Point'.

'Turning Point' was a catchy, poppy little song engineered by Chris and released as the next Stiff single. But yet again, no hit.

John did get on *Top Of The Pops* again though. Jonah Lewie had just got his 'Stop The Cavalry' song in the charts, and as he had no band to mime to the song, Stiff made one up out of whoever they could get. It was another chance to get on telly, so Otway was eager.

"That was great," says John. "When we got to the TV Centre we were told we could pick whatever instrument we fancied to mime with. I picked the drums, 'cause I reckoned I could pose the most with those. Mind you, Jonah kept telling me off 'cause I'd occasionally hit one by accident and when I did, it was always out of time. He said that it put him off."

Two flops and it was back with Barrett again, sadly just after Willy had run out of money and sold his studio, so there was nowhere for them to try out more recording.

They did put together an interesting show, called 'The Band Behind The Curtain'. Willy and John played in front of a large screen with the rest of the band behind. By using different coloured lights at different heights behind the band, musicians could be featured in coloured silhouettes during the numbers. It worked really nicely, but it was quite a costly show to do, and far too expensive to take to America – which is what Otway wanted to do, and Barrett certainly didn't.

"Christ, that guy's difficult to work with," said Otway after Willy had yet again said no to the USA. And so Chris Burkett joined the Otway band and they boarded yet another Jumbo to have another go.

Back they came after another arduous tour to similar sized audiences. "I've got to get Willy out there," said Otway. "It looks like that's the only way we'll make it big." And so it was back together with Willy yet again.

Madness were doing a UK tour and Otway and Barrett were asked if they would like to do the opening spot. It was a strange mixture of the nutty boys and the nutters, but it was good for John and Willy to play in large venues again and with a few exceptions, the duo went down well.

For this tour, they had some T-shirts printed with 'Otway and Barrett reunion, split, reunion, split, reunion, split, reunion, split, reunion, split,' with all but the first four words crossed out.

After the Madness tour, John and Willy were offered a spot on Radio One, as guest artists on the Richard Skinner show. They were to do three numbers as well as a few jingles. It was the start of a long saga that would give Otway his last near-hit.

Willy had a friend at his local pub who, after one too many lagers, would bang his head against the bar and other objects saying, "Give it headbutts". It was the sort of behaviour that reminded Willy of Otway at his best. An idea started to form in his mind about writing a song and getting John to bang his head. "I don't know if I want to do this headbutting song," said John. "It sounds both a bit silly and a little painful."

But Willy was adamant that Otway was good at these sort of things, and that they should try it out at the forthcoming radio show. John reluctantly agreed and helped by adding a couple of verses to the two that Willy already had.

Just so that you are aware of quite how silly this song was, it is worth printing some of the lines.

Lots of people in a line
Waiting for a number nine
Not me, I don't
I walk right up to the front
Excuse me are you jumping the queue?
No I'm butting in.

Walking on the beach in a force ten gale
And I saw three hippies saving a whale
I give them headbutts
Now they've gone back to India to get their heads together.

They also wrote a headbutting jingle to promote Richard Skinner's show. "I don't have to bang my head for the radio," John insisted. But Willy would have none of it. In order to get John to both get the butts right, and get the "Ow!"s in the right place, Willy held John's head firmly under his arm and banged it hard against a microphone whenever he needed a butt and an "Ow!".

"Sometimes Otway would cheat and go 'Ow!' before I banged it," says Willy. "Well it hurt just thinking about the butts," says John.

That session went well, and Willy was right about the popularity of the song. Soon listeners were writing in to Richard Skinner to ask for repeats of the headbutt jingle.

Because of the success of the Madness tour, Maurice had got Willy and John a tour supporting Squeeze. Willy insisted that they do 'Headbutts' as the final number in the set. And so as a finale to each performance Willy would lock John's head under his arm and, using that part of Otway's body as a percussion instrument, recite the headbutting song.

The audience loved it, John hated it. When John's head bled a little, the audience loved it even more, and John hated it even more.

"I can remember The Rainbow gig in London with Squeeze," says John. "It had come towards the end of 'Headbutts', and Willy yells, 'What did I give him?' and two thousand people screamed back at the top of their voices, 'A Headbutt'. It was real Romans and Christians stuff, you know with the thumbs down. I had a permanent scab on my forehead for that tour, and every night Willy would knock it off."

"It's got to be the next single," said Willy. And John had this dread. For once he could picture a hit and didn't like what he saw. He was obliged to play 'Really Free' at every gig, as it was his hit, and he loved that. The thought of being obliged to hurt his head every night was something different. "Maurice, don't let Willy persuade you to put that song out," John begged.

It appeared to Otway at this point that he had luck on his side. Willy had problems. He had just split up with his girlfriend, and though he had found another they had nowhere to live. He was also broke and in debt. Summonses from all sorts of unpaid bills kept finding him, and bailiffs had started to follow the Otway and Barrett tours.

"I might be interested in going to America," Willy said one day as yet another bailiff told him that he could find himself in jail if he didn't pay up. "But there would be the following conditions. You pay for my girlfriend to go over and pay all her expenses, you pay all my expenses, you clear up my tax bill and you guarantee that I get a decent wage while I'm over there."

Otway was ecstatic. "Do you really really think he'll come?" he said to Maurice. "I think he might, but he might change his mind at the last minute if he finds some money," Maurice replied.

Stiff were willing to put an LP out in America for this tour, and Maurice had sorted out a sleeve that would still work whether Willy came or not.

"That was dreadful," Willy remembers. "Maurice showed me the artwork for my approval. The artwork was on one sheet of card opened out before it was folded into a sleeve. The names Otway and Barrett and photos of both of us were on it, but when you folded it up into a sleeve, my name and my photos all disappeared to the back of the cover, while Otway's all stayed on the front. I couldn't get the photos changed but I did manage to get my name on the front eventually."

"It was not until Willy and his girlfriend Rose were actually on the plane that either me or Roadie Lee really believed he was coming," says John.

Roadie Lee was at this point between mega-tours and, for reasons best known to himself, fancied a spot of low life touring.

The first date on that tour was a huge festival called The Police Picnic, headlined by the hugely popular band The Police. "I was really pleased to get that," said John. "It was a great way to start that tour in front of tens of thousands of people, I thought it must be an omen." It probably was, but not in the way John was hoping.

It was a boiling hot day and the organisers had set up stalls near the front of the stage selling water-melons. By the second verse of the first Otway Barrett number, the first few slices of fruit had landed on the stage. As a response to their first number a barrage of water-melon hit the stage.

During the second number, The Police's drum kit began looking more and more like a greengrocers stall, and more and more unplayable. It began looking as if Otway and Barrett were going to spoil the Police's set as well as their own. After they had finished the second number, they were physically removed from the stage.

"I thought you said they liked you over here," said Willy, as they were being driven to a small radio studio at the festival to do an interview about their performance.

"Very occasionally I have seen acts go down as badly as yours," the interviewer began to a rather sad Otway, who was removing melon pips from his hair. "What I have never seen however is someone go down so badly so quickly. That must be one hell of a bad show you guys have got."

A few days later, Phil Evans, an Otway fan from England who was now living in Ottawa, introduced John to his next-door neighbour, a pretty 22-year-old girl called Patrice Stinson.

Patrice was the daughter of the Vice President of Bell Canada, the Canadian telephone company.

It was love at first sight, and John was as bad if not worse than he'd been over Lisa all those years before. There was a difference though. This time John's love was reciprocated. Patrice skived off work for the three days John had left in Canada, and the pair of them acted like teenagers. When they left Canada and headed into America, Otway was morose and sat in the back of the van and sulked.

"Either he was in the back of the van necking with Patrice, or he was on his own being moody," remembers Roadie Lee. "It was not very pleasant at all."

America was just as Willy had imagined it to be, and exactly the opposite to how John had described it to him. On this tour they were doing the same sorts of distances that Otway had done on previous tours, but Willy was the only driver who managed to clock up over a thousand miles in 24 hours.

Otway was in love, melancholy and writing songs. All he could talk about was getting back to Canada. It was all he could write about too.

What the hell am I doing in Champagne Illanois
When I want to be in Montreal.
I just phoned the agency
From a mid-west American city,
She said, "Tomorrow you're in Chicago
And the next day in Detroit"
And I said, "Don't bother telling me that
I ain't too interested
I just want to know
How long it is before we cross the border."
So tell me when we're playing in Montreal
'Cause there's a friend I want to see
And I hope she wants to see me
And it's hard to think of anything else at all.

"I was pleased with that song," Otway says, "it really summed up how I felt at the time."

When they were in New York, desperation had set in, so when they had a couple of days off John persuaded Willy to drive him to Ottawa, a mere eight hundred miles out of their way. "Hadn't we better wait for the work permits for Canada to get sorted out first though?" asked Willy. "No we'll blag our way through immigration, it'll be OK," said John. Which of course it wasn't.

After a nine-hour drive to the Canadian border they were turned back by an official who used very similar lines to Willy.

"I think you'd better wait for the work permits for Canada to get sorted out."

It was far too late to drive back to New York City, so the van headed for Buffalo, a boring place in comparison to the Big Apple, where they were stuck until the paper work was sorted out. "John was not very popular then," says Lee.

Otway spent the same amount of time talking to Patrice on the phone as he would have spent with her had they made it to Ottawa, and the phone bill at the motel ate deeply into Willy's wages.

Eventually they did get into Canada where John attempted, with partial success, to get Willy to drive back to Ottawa after each gig.

When they were together, John and Patrice were happy. John told her how he was a star in England with a hit record, how they made documentaries of him, and how happy they would be if they could enjoy his stardom together in the UK.

Love meant that all thoughts of cracking the States and international success were temporarily forgotten, as was any thought of his financial position. It was a long gruelling tour, as hard as any John had done in the past. It also cost a fortune, and would be the last proper tour of the States he would do.

CHAPTER
29

While Otway had been out of the country, Maurice had sorted out the release of 'Headbutts'. For once John and a record company were in agreement. Neither Stiff nor Otway wanted 'Headbutts' released. Maurice started to agree with Willy. As the song was now the highlight of the set and was being requested on the Richard Skinner show, it was worth putting out, even if that meant Maurice had to form his own label to put it on.

The label he started was Stiff Indie. He thought that this song was the sort of record that Stiff should be putting out and decided to make a point. He nicked the 'Green Green Grass Of Home' cover that Stiff had nicked from Tom Jones, crossed out the song title and wrote 'Headbutts' and added 'Indie' after the word Stiff. You can imagine the sort of reaction this had with the real record company. Predictably it was the end of them as John's label.

But 'Headbutts' did start selling. Record companies can get details of the charts up to the Top 200 and soon Otway and Barrett were in the bottom half of it. In fact, that's where they were when a love-sick star landed at Heathrow, and John resigned himself to the years of Headbutting he has done since.

Back in England, John could think of nothing but Patrice. He split up with Kathy and went back to Aylesbury for a while. From Ash Grove he called Patrice, asked her to give up her good job as a commercial artist and move over to England. She was as besotted as he was and agreed.

John did not want to ask his parents if he could move Patrice as well as himself into Ash Grove, and was desperate to find a love nest for himself and his sweetheart. Maurice came to the rescue. Morgan Fisher, John's old keyboard player, was on tour with Queen for a few months, and Maurice persuaded him to lend John his luxury flat in the smart part of Notting Hill Gate.

John picked up Patrice at Heathrow Airport and took her back to his new flat. He was trying to impress her, and it would seem he succeeded. "Queen's keyboard player, a friend of mine, has lent us his flat for a while," he said, as he introduced her to their new home.

That night John proposed. He had spent a total of 14 days with this young girl, and was sure he wanted to marry her and spend the rest of his life with her. She must have been impressed, as she agreed immediately and ran off to phone her mum with the news.

John and Patrice married within a week of her landing in Britain. John was about to tour Ireland with Willy and suggested it would be good to marry beforehand as they could use the Irish tour as a honeymoon.

They decided on a quiet wedding. Willy and Lee were invited, as was Maurice and his girlfriend. "But no publicity," said John. "This is a highly personal thing, and I don't know how to break it to my parents so I think I'll tell them after the event, when I think the time's right."

Maurice was having none of this. It had been hard getting air play on 'Headbutts', as the BBC foolishly thought it was a violent song. Maurice judged, accurately, that John getting married might just warrant a Radio One play, and the men at the BBC were well aware of the forthcoming event.

On returning to England, Willy, since he had nowhere to live, had bought another coach. Having no fixed abode was a handy way of escaping the inevitable bailiffs. The Otways' wedding ceremony was made more normal by the lack of Wild Willy, who missed it trying to find a parking spot for the coach.

It was the other things that made this day special for John and Patrice. One of them was the play 'Headbutts' got on Radio One, with special congratulations from the BBC. John knew what effect this would have on a whole host of people he hadn't warned, his family amongst them. They were now getting endless calls from well-wishers and hadn't a clue what they were on about. Chris France was pretty shocked too, and immediately sent a letter to Potter, who had given up on Otway long before this and got a job in Saudi Arabia.

Another special thing that day was the wedding night. Yes, Otway did a gig on his wedding night, a BBC *In Concert* programme. John and Willy played a special version of 'Headbutts' with a verse for the bride. It was Patrice's first indication of what marriage to a rock star, at least marriage to Otway, was like. There was worse to come. Much worse.

The first day of The Honeymoon Tour was fine. As a wedding present, Maurice had flown the happy couple first-class to Dublin, and put them in a nice hotel.

But while the newly-weds were enjoying the luxury of British Airways special services, and the romance of a four-star hotel, Wild Willy was driving over a clapped-out VW camper with no heater to join them.

For some, rock and roll tours have a certain ring of glamour. Maurice's special economy tours do not. That December the weather dropped well below freezing and the snow was reminiscent of the Canadian winters Patrice thought she had left behind.

The second Otway gig that Patrice saw as his wife was in Cork, a three-hour journey from Dublin in the icy camper, into a dressing room that the previous band had knocked the window out of.

About three days into wedded bliss, Patrice asked John about his financial status and how much wealth he had accumulated over his years of stardom. "Well, I reckon at the moment," he said thoughtfully, "that give or take a couple of grand, I'm about 30 thousand in debt."

After the Irish tour, John went back over the Atlantic, to meet his in-laws and to spend Christmas in Canada. Maurice phoned him there to tell him that 'Headbutts' had gone up to 76 in the charts. It was a popular record, and if 'DK 50/80' was bought for the wrong reasons, then it was John's only other successful single.

Sadly, being on a small independent label, and with minimal BBC play because of the violent nature of the song, 'Headbutts' remained at 76 for a further five weeks, never quite managing to make it into the Top 75.

Back in England, Otway tried to get back in the studio with Willy to capitalise on their recent single success. But it wasn't working very well. John and Willy had this time been together a total of four months, which included an American tour. It was a remarkable achievement for them not to split up during this time, but to all who knew them, it was obvious that something would trigger another separation. "It was probably Otway recording an album with someone else, and calling it 'All Balls And No Willy'," suggests Maurice.

John had got together with a band called The Europeans, who had supported the duo on a number of dates in the last few months. They rehearsed and recorded a batch of songs he had either written with Chris Burkett, or written for Patrice.

By now, no major label would touch Otway product and so Maurice put the LP out on a label he'd formed called Empire

Records. Although the title of the record tended to raise a smile, it did not help to get it on to the shelves of Boots and W.H.Smiths and it was doomed to become Otway's least selling LP (unless he chooses to make another that is).

John was really stuck for money, and completely clueless as to what he could do with his career. He knew America had not worked for him and a year was spent in the mental wilderness while Otway wondered how on earth destiny was going to make it for him.

Debts had risen to an alarming proportion, so bad in fact that John had given up his Maida Vale 'star's' flat, and he and Patrice had to move back to Aylesbury to live with John's parents. Living with John's Mum and Dad was possibly not what Patrice had in mind when she moved to England. Neither did she imagine that she would end up with the job of unpaid roadie.

Back in Aylesbury, John started to work with Robin Boult. He was one of the best local guitarists, and had been around since the days of the *The Bell Magazine* and *The Roxette*.

In a small 1,300cc Austin A40 car, with an enclosed coffin-like roof-rack almost as big as the car itself, John, Patrice and Robin toured the country doing one-night gigs. Patrice was both driver and roadie as Robin at this point could not drive. Sometimes they would travel as far as Newcastle and back in the same night. It was not a satisfactory situation.

During this period of worry and searching, though, things were changing. By the end of it, John would have a new motto and rule by which to run his life. "If I can't get a gold record, I'll go for the Oscar."

CHAPTER 30

While John was in Canada, Gary Topp (one of two Garys to help John in that country, and who still liked him even after the Police Picnic) suggested that John should play at a comedy club in Toronto called Yuk Yuks.

Over the years, Otway's performances had relied more and more on John's absurd sense of humour. He had learned which of the stupid things he did made audiences laugh, so that what had started as sheer over-the-top physical and vocal mayhem had become fractionally more refined and funnier. It's as if it was his 'silly singing' coming of age.

At Yuk Yuks John found himself on a bill with only stand-up comedians. He had put together a short set of the most amusing of his material, and shocked himself by going down better than any of them. What had been blatantly obvious for decades, suddenly became obvious to John himself. "I can't really sing, people come to see me because it's a good laugh."

With this brilliant flash of insight, John knew that stardom was more likely as a comedian than a singer. "You mean you want to be more like Benny Hill!" said Maurice, as John tried to explain this to him.

Following this revelation, Otway added more and more touches of his brand of humour. He sawed up two of his own Gibson guitars and hinged them together with a neck pointing in each direction, and called it the Gibson Ambidextrous, "because I play right and left-handed guitars as bad as each other."

He took apart an electronic drum machine, and made pads that triggered off the various drum sounds. By attaching these to his body, he could hit himself and sound like a drummer. By bouncing his bottom on the stage at the same time, he could 'go around the kit' as it were. Otway liked this, and with a certain amount of experiment discovered that simulated sex with an amplifier sounded like a fair copy of a Keith Moon solo.

As well as Yuk Yuks, Gary Topp managed to get Otway to play in a club in New York on a comedy night, supporting a group called The Wow Show. This was our star's introduction to alternative comedy, and John thought there might well be an opening in this new form of entertainment for him.

Back in England, John met up with The Wow Show again, and asked them if he could do a bit in the next show that they did. "If I can do a bit of comedy," John told them, "I don't mind coming on and playing my hit."

It was agreed, and Otway joined them for three weeks at The Latchmere Theatre in Battersea. The group gave John a few lines in a couple of sketches, he got a few laughs and immediately knew that he was a natural actor.

Within weeks of John coming to terms with his new-found abilities, he was producing, writing and directing his own half-hour sit-coms and committing them to video, taking his new more theatrical act up to Edinburgh Fringe Festival and making a video to sell mail order and at gigs.

John had persuaded Gordon Gilbert, a local chap who had a video studio near Aylesbury, to film him doing his various sitcoms and ideas with the promise that there would be rich returns from selling the videos. John put together a short 17-minute selection of songs and called it *The Nearly Free Video*.

It was an interesting piece of work, the most interesting thing about it being the way the actual videos were made. John built a machine that could wind 10 videos from one three-hour tape. The winding onto the empty cassette cases was done with a hand drill with a bolt in the end: 23 turns of the drill produced one *Nearly Free* video.

In the end it was a bit like John's first attempts at running a record company. More of these videos were given away than sold, and Gordon, like Chris France before him, never saw the promised fortune from the venture.

After a year at Ash Grove, Patrice had had enough of living with in-laws. As John had no money at all, she arranged for her parents to lend them enough to put the deposit on a small flat, and the couple moved back to Maida Vale.

Whilst doing The Wow Show at the Latchmere Theatre, John was introduced to the artistic director of the place, Lou Stein. John had explained that he was now seriously contemplating an acting career, and was looking for a part in a play or something in which he could be discovered. Lou liked John and auditioned him for a small part in an adaption of George Orwell's *Down And Out In Paris And London*.

It was a small part, the part of Henry, a sewer worker, and Otway struggled trying to get a French accent. In the first few weeks of rehearsal though, something appeared to be going wrong with John as a stage actor. "Whenever I rehearsed with a band," John explains, "I always saved my performance 'till there was an audience. I never saw the point in doing the somersaults or the headbutts and things if there was nobody there to impress. I did the same in the rehearsals for *Down And Out*. I learned my lines, found out where I was supposed to stand, and delivered them in a pretty dull sort of monotone."

Lou and the rest of the cast just assumed that this quirky singer was no good at acting at all, and simply gave up on him. Ronan Willmot, another actor, had noticed something in Otway, and had worked out what he was up to. "John," he said, "you're saving your performance for the first night, aren't you?" "Of course," John replied.

Ronan explained to Otway that what he was doing was unfair. "They think that's how you act," he said. "They're used to this mousey voice that no one can hear. If on the first night you suddenly come out of your shell, you will throw everybody, their mouths will fall open. The idea of rehearsal is partly to get used to the other actors and what they do."

The next day, Otway took the advice and tried out the performance he had planned to attract as much attention to the small part of Henry as possible. Sure enough, the whole cast and the director stood open-mouthed as Otway the actor delivered his lines.

There were other problems too. John was given a costume that did indeed make him look remarkably like a thirties sewer worker. The one thing that totally ruined the illusion was that John regularly forgot to remove his earrings. However, these offending pieces of jewelry disappeared from the dressing room after John was reminded to take them off for his third entrance that night. Oddly enough, no one knew where they were, and John decided, "Now I'm an actor and not a rock star I don't suppose I need them."

His part in *Down And Out* was of a size that made getting discovered highly unlikely, and Otway needed to get discovered pretty rapidly. Preferably before he went bankrupt and the new flat was repossessed.

As it happens, destiny was not planning to let Otway hit rock bottom just yet. A few things happened that made John's idea of becoming an actor almost feasible.

Paul Jackson, who had seen John at the Edinburgh Fringe Festival, and was the producer of the BBC comedy series *The Young Ones*, offered John the opportunity to do a song. It was John's first major TV appearance in ages and he planned to introduce the populace to his new more comic theatrical performance with his 'Body Talk' number. John's performance on *The Young Ones*, was neither brilliant nor bad. It didn't have the same effect as the *Whistle Test*, but Otway was determined to make of it what he could.

John knew it was unlikely that he would ever get a decent-sized part in a play, and so he did what he always did in these situations, write one himself, giving himself the star role.

Before even putting pen to paper, Otway had booked The Gate theatre in Notting Hill Gate and Theatre Workshop in Edinburgh for the Fringe festival. He then set about approaching the cast of *Down And Out* to find the actors for the supporting roles. One of these was Paul Bradley, a highly talented young man who was to do for Otway's acting what Wild Willy had done for his music.

When Otway and Bradley met to discuss Otway's play there was nothing at all in terms of a script or an idea. "The only thing he'd done was book the theatres, and decided that he wanted completely over-the-top scenery," says Paul.

"Yeah, I didn't really go for the sort of plays where you just used a bit of lighting and a few props to give the impression of a cafe in Paris or a street in London," says John. "I thought the plays we did at school were better than that, you know, where Aladdin's cave looked like a cave, and the forest had lots of painted canvas trees.

"So I thought it would be pretty neat to have something like a huge pop-up book with a scene on every page, so you could walk from one page to another through doors, and have beds that fell down from the pages as you turned them, and things like that."

Bradley was impressed, as others had been before, with Otway's ambition and enthusiasm. It was new to him, it was an unusual way for an actor to approach his profession. He had also spotted something in Otway that was as close to talent as John was ever likely to get.

"Most actors," Paul explained to John, "learn by observation. By watching how different sorts of people react, they can teach themselves to feel what they feel and find within themselves enough of that person so that, when they come to act, they are convincing. You, however, do not observe anything. Everything you act is a straight extension of yourself. But that is not always a disadvantage, a lot of actors get type-cast in one sort of part anyway.

"If you stick to parts like village idiots, loonies and amiable dim-bats, you could go far. Your performances would be convincing, because in your case, you would be that loony or dim-bat."

Most people would have probably been offended by such words, but not Otway. He immediately went home and started writing a part for himself as Gordon, a bit of a Wally.

Paul also explained to John that the most important thing to an actor after an Equity card, (which Otway had got since the days of his hit, when he believed that Hollywood was just around the corner) were agents and casting directors. Paul helped John to put together a CV, got him to get some photographs done that did not have him with microphones in his mouth, hanging upside down, doing somersaults or giving headbutts, and gave him a list of people to send them to.

Some of these were to become very helpful to John's acting career, Maureen Vincent from the Frazer and Dunlop Agency, and John and Roz Hubbard from Hubbard's Casting in particular.

Both called Otway in for interviews. Maureen expressed a certain interest and the Hubbards said that they would put him up for some TV adverts that they were casting.

Meanwhile, Otway and Bradley were working on their play. As with other things John had done in the past, as long as he got the starring role, he did not really mind what anyone else did. Paul fancied playing two completely different characters and it worked out that they both wrote pretty much their own parts for themselves. They got in two other actors, Simon Roberts, who was playing the lead in *Down And Out*, and Tootsie Roll, a vivacious young actress that Lou Stein had introduced them to.

Verbal Diary, as the play was called, was a success. It was a success for a number of reasons. John could be very funny, and he was funny in this. Bradley directed it (he had to, as John had no idea how to) with an uncanny understanding of the Otway humour which he balanced brilliantly with his own.

But the most outstanding part of this show was probably the set, the eight by seven-foot page 'pop-up' book that John had so dearly wanted.

It was designed and built by Bettina Dix and Paul's brother Ciaran. Bettina was a friend of Paul's and a set designer. She too had worked with plays whose scenery was largely governed by small budgets and welcomed Otway's extravagant ideas as a bit of a challenge. The problem with ideas like this though is the amount they cost. This was solved by reverting back to the theory that no problem is too big as long as one can borrow enough money to solve it. Rik Mayall, of *Young Ones* fame, was an old university buddy of Paul's, and he kindly invested enough money in the new theatrical company to get it built.

"Bettina and Ciaran were amazing," says John. "We met them and went through all the things we wanted, like the pop-up bed, doors that went from the bedroom page to the living room page, a pub page with pop-out bar, a bathroom page with pop-out shower and a pop-up spiral staircase."

As odd as it may seem, out of all these requests, only the spiral staircase proved an impossibility. And the four of them together devised extra set jokes, like half the cast getting stuck between the pages of the living room as Gordon hurried to the bathroom page to go to the loo.

Simon and Tootsie got caught up in the enthusiasm behind the play and added a lot, as did Liam Grundy, who was brought in to help with the music.

On opening night at The Gate Theatre, Otway knew that his gamble had paid off, as the cast took three curtain calls, and the set got a standing ovation.

"Bettina and Ciaran's book made that show work as much as anything else," says John. "When I explained what we wanted to other people, they all said it was either too expensive or impossible. Lou Stein for example said that even if the book was built it would fall through the theatre floor. Usually people laughed at my ideas, but the only thing that Bettina and Ciaran laughed at was the spiral staircase."

Sadly, they never really got paid for all the work they put in, as they were yet again the victims of Otway's, "There'll be tons of money to share out once it's a huge success."

Just when *Verbal Diary* was opening, John got his first TV commercial. Some actors are worried about doing commercials because of what it might do to their credibility. Not Otway, he loved the idea. "It gets me on telly a lot," was his reaction.

Toshiba wanted a rather over-the-top sax player and bass player to advertise their stereos. He did not have to play these instruments, just pose with them, which was just as well as Otway could play neither. But he could pose with both pretty adeptly, so adeptly in fact that he had all the people at the casting session laughing. John even found he liked these sort of auditions – it didn't matter if he got the parts, it was just another chance to show off.

After Hubbard's Casting rang Otway with the good news, he phoned Frazer and Dunlop and asked them to sort out the contract for him. It was the start of a very fruitful liaison.

Maureen Vincent from the company was curious about John and came down to see his new play.

"Maureen wasn't the only one," recalls John. "One night at The Gate we had five casting directors, Maureen from Frazers, and Rik Mayall and Ade Edmondson from *The Young Ones*."

Eventually everyone in the cast got work from doing that show. and Otway to this day considers it one of the few achievements of which he is truly proud. "Well there are not that many of them," he laughs.

CHAPTER 31

The Toshiba advert was the start of a year of our star's life dominated by TV commercials. "It was a really exciting year," says John. "I never seemed to be off the box. People were always coming up to me and saying that they had seen me on telly last night."

Paul Bradley had been right about the sort of parts Otway could do. The parts he went up for, and the parts he got, were indeed all various half-wits and dim-bats. In order of appearance, they were:

The wild miming sax and bass player; the chap who had to ring a problem line because he was a secret lemonade drinker, and then dances out of the phone box singing about it (however it was decided that John's voice was not quite 'right', and so Otway looks even more like a nerd with a good singing voice coming out of his uncoordinated body); the embarrassing relation at a wedding where a nice English boy is marrying into a Mafia family. (Otway walks up to the bride's father and says "Don, I can call you Don, can't I? What gets me is what your daughter sees in him. He's hardly Al Cappuccino is he?"); a lab technician, whose job it is to count pieces of toast as they come out of a toaster, a job he cannot do without burning his fingers; and finally, Danepak bacon had John falling over a cliff, first in a tent and then in a camper van, as he tries to cook his breakfast, with the line, "When it comes to saving your skin or saving your bacon".

Apart from being on TV a lot, there were other things that Otway loved about doing these commercials. Two of them were filmed in Italy, and John loved the first class flights, the good hotels and especially being treated like a star. It was almost as good as the days of the Bentley and a good deal better than the tours Maurice organised.

Every time Otway got one of these commercials he would find out the first time it was due to be on TV and invite all his friends around for a party and to watch him on the box. Les Gray was invited to one of these and remembers it vividly.

"Yeah, we all went round to Otway's flat for the party, which would have been quite good fun if John hadn't rushed around every quarter of an hour yelling, 'The adverts are on, The adverts are on,' and we'd all have to gather around the telly to watch them. The trouble was, John had got the day wrong. We spent a few hours watching the adverts 'till we all got terribly bored and headed down to the pub. Mind you, when the pub closed we all had to go back and watch the video and check all the commercial breaks to see if he was on."

Maurice had put out a version of 'Middle Of Winter', which John had recorded with Robin. As with all his recent records it got nowhere.

"Now I'm an actor, I don't need a manager anymore," John told Maurice one day. As attempting to organise John's career was far more work than reward, Maurice most heartily agreed, and Maurice and John shook hands on it before Otway had a chance to change his mind. "Yes, I suppose at that point I was doing well as an actor," says John.

Such was the unanimity of this agreement that the two have remained firm friends ever since. "I don't know if I'd ever want to manage him again though," says Maurice grinning.

Apart from the times when John was acting in commercials, the gigging up and down the country continued. The little A40 with the roof-rack had decided that it was carrying a little too much weight and actually split in half three miles outside Aylesbury. The rock and roll vehicle was upgraded to a Ford Cortina Estate. Apart from this small improvement in travelling standards, life for the Otways continued to be four nights a week travelling, headbutting and travelling again.

John did find himself a new agent for the music side of his career, Neil Smith, who managed to boost John's earnings from gigs considerably. With this money and the money from adverts, the mortgage got paid up to date and it looked incredibly as if Otway was slowly getting back on his feet. The £30,000 debt was still there, but it had stopped growing.

Chris France had not been idle meanwhile. Possibly after driving John's Bentley he had decided that there may be money to be made out of the music business. He had started managing Warren Harry (the chap Otway had disqualified from his school talent competition). Warren was now writing songs and Chris had sent some to Andy Hill, the producer of Bucks Fizz. Amongst them was the hit 'When We Were Young'.

Very soon, Chris was working from the Bucks Fizz offices in Piccadilly Circus. After the Bradford Football Club fire disaster, the Fizz office called John. A version of 'You'll Never Walk Alone' was being recorded on the same basis as the Band Aid single. Bucks Fizz had been asked to help, but were unable to, so Chris had suggested Otway.

In this way, John got to join a band called The Crowd for a day, with such people as The Nolans, Bruce Forsyth and Gerry Marsden, and have a number one hit record.

Half-way through 1986 Otway got his first real acting role, a large part in two episodes of William Tell playing a character called Conrad, William's friend.

When they were casting this part they were looking for an amusing awkward person to contrast a strong agile William. Many actors were auditioned for this part, but none proved amusing or awkward enough until the casting director Debbie McWilliams called in John for the part.

The casting session was first thing in the morning and our disorganised hero had copied down the wrong address. On the day in question, Debbie, who had known John and Patrice since the days of Verbal Diary, discovered John two doors away from her Soho office, ringing a door bell marked 'Jane, model and French lessons'. After saying hello, she realised what he was doing, blushed and said, "Oh I'm terribly sorry I shouldn't have really seen you here, should I?" John explained that he was due to meet her and the director, not a model, and she whisked him away out of trouble.

Otway first thing in the morning is the perfect definition of the word awkward, especially after he bangs his head on the way in to the office and empties the whole contents of his shoulder bag on the floor whilst shaking hands with the director. He was given the part on the spot.

So excited was everyone to find someone possessing Otway's unique talents that no one bothered to ask him if he could ride a horse. "I thought it was funny," says John, "'cause when I checked the scripts there was a line for me to say while I was on a horse. It was only one short line, so I thought I'd just have to sit on top of the animal and say it, no problem."

That one short scene would be the first scene to be shot, and Otway's introduction to TV stardom. There was a long track leading up to a castle. Across this track the director drew a line with a stick, and said to Conrad and William, "OK, if you can just gallop up to here, not a really fast gallop, stop, do your lines and gallop off into the distance, that'd be great."

After this a very scared Otway was introduced to and placed upon Oscar, Conrad's horse. "The bloody thing was a film stunt horse," remembers John with remarkable clarity. "The beast knew how to act better than I did. As soon as the director yelled 'roll cameras' it started getting excited. As he yelled 'mark it' and it heard the click of the clapper board it was ready to go. On hearing the word 'action', it was off and galloping, expecting to leap hedges or ravines.

"Luckily, William's horse and Oscar knew each other, and so both stopped at the same time. I managed to get my line out before Oscar galloped away with me again, and thought 'Thank God that's over'. It wasn't.

"As me and Oscar were caught and brought back, the director said, 'That was awful, you looked as if you were going to a funeral.' We had to do that scene 14 times before we got it right: stopping in the right place doing the lines and me looking happy enough. My bum was so sore that for the whole two weeks we were filming I had to sleep on my stomach."

Otway had a stunt double for this programme. There was a lot of complicated sword fighting in one of the episodes, and this chap and William's double had spent a week carefully preparing and rehearsing a fight sequence. It was a complicated fight, a huge two-ton swinging blade on a pendulum swishing to and fro between the two swordsmen in a battle to the death.

John had already upset his double. When they first met, his double (who had an obviously expensive designer haircut) had looked in horror at Otway's £3.50 barber job, realising that he would have to have his crowning glory massacred in a similar manner.

John watched the fight scene with interest before pointing out to his double that he was in fact left-handed. In the end, it turned out that our hero was not a natural swordsman and, in Otway's hands, a blade would have looked just as awkward if he had it in his right foot.

It is a shame the British public never got to see Otway's awkward portrayal of Conrad. The series was taken off the air the week before John's episodes were to be shown. As far as we know, this was not so much because John was in them, but more that a series of serious crimes had been committed using crossbows.

1986 also found John another starring TV role in a children's programme called *Supergran*. It was the sort of part that was made for our star. He was such an obvious choice for the part that Tyne Tees Television did not even need to audition him. The episode was called *Supergran And The Chronic Crooner*, and no sooner had his agents sent up copies of his records than the part was his.

The only problem John encountered with this part was the Birmingham accent that the Chronic Crooner was supposed to have. John doing accents was an amazing speedy geography lesson. "He could cover the whole of England, Ireland, Scotland and Wales in one sentence," recalls Tim Dowd, the director.

Apart from this major hitch, John's performance as the Chronic Crooner was a piece of television magic. He had to do things like sing so badly out of tune that those listening were forced to block up their ears. No 14 takes this time. On action, Otway performed his discordant singing to perfection. As part of the plot, he had to think that what he was doing sounded perfectly alright. He had been doing this all his life and played that to perfection too.

At the end of that show, the Chronic Crooner has the lines: "See, the thing is Supergranny Supersmith, show business is all I know. I mean (sniff) what else can you do when you're useless, brainless and talentless eh?"

It was a touching moment, and probably John's finest piece of acting so far, with disturbing and uncanny parallels between the character he was playing and Otway himself.

Brian Eastman, a film producer, had seen John playing at a club. He had enjoyed the performance and been impressed with the way that John could get away with using the strangest combinations of words in his songs. He liked the way Otway could have a song in which the chorus line went, 'Beware of the flowers 'cause I'm sure they're going to get you yeah", and actually make it fit.

He was producing a movie called *Whoops Apocalypse*, and came to see if John could possibly come up with the title song. It was an interesting problem to get the words 'Whoops Apocalypse' into the chorus of a song, but John discovered that the tune and rhythm of 'Big Country' – Boom, da da da dah – fitted neatly with the words 'Whoops A-po-ca-lypse', and based his song on this theory. Brian must have been either impressed or amused as Otway got his song picked as the theme tune to the film.

Towards the end of that year, John made another recording – the William Blake hymn, 'Jerusalem'. It is one hundred per cent classic Otway.

Liam Grundy, who had done the music for *Verbal Diary*, had often caught John singing to himself. It was something Otway had always done, and if it was not something he was trying to write himself, it would be the strangest mixture of songs and tunes imaginable. Nothing was stranger than John's personal version of 'Jerusalem' – there were beats missing all over the place, and where John was unable to sing notes he had changed the tune. It sounded attractive though, nothing like the massed choir version, but almost plaintive and folky. Liam, off his own back, booked a studio and invited John to have a go at doing a recording of it. Everyone agreed that it sounded good, some even said it was good enough to be a Christmas hit. The idea of a "hit before Christmas", still appealed to John, even John the actor.

John rang Chris France at the Bucks Fizz office to tell him that he had a hit record and could Chris sort out a deal with a major label to handle it for him. Chris heard the record, and thought that it was worth a go, even though he was in the process of changing offices and jobs. He had teamed up with a DJ, Simon Harris, and was starting his own dance label. However, Otway was an old mate, and if he could help him get another hit to go with the one he had, he would.

All the major labels were approached, and quickly, as time was running out to get it released before Christmas. Soon Chris had received rejections from all but one of them, WEA.

Paul Conroy was the unfortunate A&R man at WEA. He had known John from Stiff records, and called Chris saying, "It's quite interesting, let me play it to a few people and I'll let you know."

A comment of this nature was enough to set Otway off on one of his "Hit Before Christmas" speeches, bringing back memories of days gone by and the nostalgia of The Derby Arms.

Days went by though, and Paul Conroy had not 'let them know'. Chris was used to the music business by this time, and knew that it was a sure sign that WEA did not want to put out Otway's record. "Well can't we make them?" asked Otway.

No one had ever 'made' a major corporation put out a record before. Otway was about to. The following press release, issued by John and Chris, tells the story quite adequately:

JOHN OTWAY SIGNS WEA

Usually these days it is the record companies who sign artists, but in this case – Otway has decided to sign a major record company! Usually the record company pay an artist an advance on record sales – Otway is paying WEA an advance on record sales! Usually record companies have a choice in which records they release – Otway is trying his hardest to make sure they don't! Having heard that several people in the company liked his version of 'The New Jerusalem', Otway rushed out and ordered two thousand records with WEA labels (copied from a ZZ Top record), and is presenting them to the company on November 6. "I suppose they are going to be shocked when they suddenly receive all these records they didn't know they were releasing," says Otway. "And the advance will not mean a great deal to a company of that size, but the contract I have sent them is a fair one. I honestly love the record and believe it needs a major company to deal with it. I am giving them as much help as I can, getting the records to all the papers, TV and radio stations."

"I really liked that little scheme of John's," Chris says. "Mind you, as with all his schemes it was expensive. First of all, we worked out that no company, apart from WEA, would dare press records with a WEA label on them, so we had the singles pressed with blank labels and got a dodgy printer to print the labels on self-adhesive paper.

"I spent ages looking for a WEA label to copy before finding this ZZ Top record. It cost a mint to get a proper graphic artist to change the name of the song and put Otway's name on, but the finished thing did look like a proper WEA record. The other funny thing we did was pick the serial number OTWEA 1 for the record.

"Because we were signing a record company, Otway insisted on me getting him a top music business lawyer to make up a contract. That cost a mint too."

On November 6, 1986, Chris had in his office two thousand copies of the 'WEA' record, press releases, and the contract with which Otway was to sign his new company. Tony Bramwell, who after dealing with Otway's stunts at Polydor was delighted to see John having a go at another company, quite happily took the record around to Radio One a few hours before WEA were presented with box after box after box of their new single, a contract and a picture cheque (yes Otway still had them) for £200 made payable to WEA.

"I suppose they could have sued us," says John, "But luckily the media, as well as me, liked the idea of the desperate artist signing the big label and by lunchtime Paul Conroy phoned to say that WEA would, in fact, allow themselves to be signed by me and would put the record out."

By the time Otway came to terms with the fact that 'The New Jerusalem' was not going to be a hit, he had already celebrated its success on successive nights in expensive restaurants, bought endless bottles of champagne and, as with Polydor before, was almost working nine to five in the various departments of the corporation he had just signed. Apart from his continual presence in the building, WEA found that there were other disadvantages in being signed by Otway. Firstly, he demanded things like expensive photo sessions and secondly, he did not sell any records.

You would have thought that after this, WEA would have had no more to do with our star's career, but Otway had his foot in the door of a major company and the corporation were doomed to release yet another single before John was to find himself yet again 'between labels'.

Whoops Apocalypse was coming out as a movie the following spring. "Look what hits 'I Was Born Under A Wandering Star',

'Live And Let Die', 'Ghostbusters' and other songs from films are," John told WEA.

And Otway was correct. In that year of 1987 the song 'I Want To Be Your Drill Instructor', from the film *Full Metal Jacket*, was a huge hit.

Unfortunately, his 'Whoops Apocalypse' based loosely on the Big Country theme was not. But WEA took the gamble and promised to put it out and see if there was any reaction. There was none. In fact it is the only Otway record to get no air play at all.

After getting the producer, Brian Eastman, to lend him the use of the film's footage to make a video, Otway hounded his record company to fund it. "Listen Otway," they said impatiently, "we don't mind making a video if you sell some records. But if we can't even get you on the radio, do you really think we're going to get you on TV?"

"If my telly appearances sell gammon steaks and bacon grills, I'm sure they're going to sell my records," said John. But WEA were adamant. No budget for a video.

"I've got a few million quid's worth of footage towards my video, and no one will help me finish it," complained Otway bitterly to everyone. Eventually, Paul Bradley introduced John to Iain Softly and Roger Brown, a director and producer respectively, with whom Otway's "I've got a few million quid's worth of footage" angle paid off, and they agreed to make the video for him.

Iain came up with a simple story line: Otway looking for a cheap way to record a video. He spots a presenter doing some outside broadcast in a park and butts in. He steals the film from a cinema. He notices a plugged-in home video camera in a shop window and sings into that. Finally, he goes around to the Channel 4 TV offices and sings in their Video Box. It was a good script for a video and Steve Blacknell and Rik Mayall both turned up to help John make it free of charge.

As it was approaching April 1, Otway decided to present his record company with his video and a bill for £117,000 as a joke. He also managed to get *Music Week* magazine to print the following little snippet on the same day: "Although the recent policy of major record labels has been to wait for a record to enter the *Music Week* Top 75 before committing a huge budget to a video, an interesting exception to this rule emerged this week. John Otway, hardly one of WEA's top selling acts, has managed to extract a budget of £117,000 for a minor epic to promote his single 'Whoops Apocalypse'. 'No one was more surprised than me,' says Otway. 'However, they've recently had a great deal of singles success so they must have a bit of money to throw around on such things.' The video, as well as featuring Rik Mayall and presenter Steve Blacknell, has cameo roles from Peter Cook, Loretta Switt and Alexei Sayle. Paul Conroy, head of marketing at WEA, agreed that making the video was unusual but said that 'Otway is an unusual artist with an unusual talent. You must bear in mind,' he said, 'that the film *Whoops Apocalypse* is going on international release and we would expect the single to be a hit in more territories than just the UK.'

We will never know whether or not Otway was as good at selling records as he was bacon grills. Channel 4 were sent a copy of the new Otway video, and foolishly believed the video box sequence was taking the mickey out of their *Right To Reply* programme. "And the last thing we want is to encourage loonies like Otway to turn up singing in our video boxes," a spokesman for the programme said.

Using the fact that John was infringing their copyright, they banned the video from ever getting shown. So as well as no radio play, there was no TV play either.

CHAPTER 33

Otway at this point became disillusioned and desperate and made a series of decisions that were little short of catastrophic. "I'm going to retire from music," he said. "I'm going to become an actor and TV star."

He got Neil Smith to book his retirement tour and told the world he would gig and headbutt no more. It was not the wisest thing to do. Gigs had been John's only regular source of income over the years.

"If I give them up," John said, "then it will force me to do something else." As it indeed did.

Otway noticed that the small flat he and Patrice had bought had doubled in value in the three years that they had been there. They had a mortgage of £27,000 and the flat was now worth £60,000. The realisation that more could be made from property than headbutts was not slow in coming. "While I'm working on my acting career, I'll be a property developer," thought Otway.

The plan was simple. Sell the flat they had, pay off the most pressing of Otway's debts, keeping a large sum of money to keep them going for a year or so, and get another 90 per cent mortgage on a property that they could develop.

"Otway was really enthusiastic about this property developing idea," remembers Chris France. "He came around my office saying, 'Look mate, I've made thirty grand in three years.' I must admit to being quite impressed with that, that's how I got sucked into it."

Chris was thinking of moving to London, as his record company, Music Of Life, specialising in the new rap and hip-hop music was just taking off. John suggested that Chris, his girlfriend Karen, Patrice and himself should together buy a large flat that they could convert into two smaller ones. "That would make us thirty grand each in a year," John explained carefully to Chris, who saw no reason why this would not work.

Within three days, Otway had put his flat on the market, found a buyer and discovered their new convertable property. There was a gap of a few weeks between selling Clifton Court and buying and moving into the new place. "We need a holiday anyway," said John, who felt that being homeless for a few weeks was as good a reason as any for taking one.

The Otways went to Crete. Most people regard going to Greece as a cheap holiday, and maybe it would have been if John had not taken the nest egg "to last a year or so" with them. "But it was a bloody good holiday," remembers John.

So depleted were the funds, that upon arriving back at Victoria Station the Otways had to get a cab round to Maurice Bacon's and drag him out of bed so he could both pay the cab and lend them enough money to get home. "I'm so glad I don't manage you anymore," said Maurice as he gave Otway another tenner he would never see again.

Otway's change of career, into being a full-time professional actor, lasted three months. "John came round my house one day," says Paul Bradley, "and asked me to get another comedy thing together with him. *Verbal Diary* had worked well, and so I thought why not? Besides, he was saying there would be something like 15 shows at four hundred pounds a time over a three-week period, and we'd split the money."

John and Paul spent a couple of weeks writing and rehearsing a show, and in the end they performed it a grand total of three times. And for nothing like the money John had promised.

Life in the 'convertible' was not going too smoothly either. As Otway was getting more and more into a mess, Chris France's business was doing better and better. "It's alright you wanting to be a property developer," Chris said one day, "but how on earth are you going to pay the builders?"

John had no option. Three months after giving up music he had to come out of retirement. "Well, I'm going to come out of retirement with a bang," said Otway.

The bang that Otway had in mind was yet another reunion with Willy Barrett. "At least I know that will make a fortune," he said. "We'll do an album, a single and a tour."

Willy was worried, but said, "You pay the studio bills and guarantee the money on the tour, and I'll do it."

John begged and borrowed the £1,000 for some studio time, and he and Willy went into Pace Studios in Milton Keynes to start the new LP. At the same time, he hired a secretary to do the publicity for him, ordered 5,000 posters, and hired top photographer John Breen to take pictures of the reunion.

There was of course the question of material. Even though it had been five years since the last LP, John had hardly written a thing. He searched through all the unrecorded material he had, discovering only a wealth of soppy songs.

Willy had often jokingly referred to his partnership with Otway as "The Wimp And The Wild", and suggested that they could give the LP this title. "If we did that," he said, "we could put all that awful wet stuff you've got on one side and call it the wimp side, and any good material we've got can go on the wild side."

'The Wimp And The Wild', with Side Wimp and Side Wild, seemed like a good idea. One of John's songs, 'Losing', started with the lines:

I used to think losing was coming in last
I now know it is not
Losing is not being able to find
Something you know you have got

It was regarded as so soppy by Wild Willy, that he insisted that it should be the title song for one side and called simply 'The Wimp'. Willy collaborated with John to write a song called 'The Wild' to get the other side going.

Cheryl Farthing, the girl John had employed to do the publicity, was having problems on two fronts. One, John was having difficulties paying her wages, and was even borrowing the odd fiver off her, and two, the mass media did not seem to be very interested in the 'reunion of the decade'.

Neil Smith, the agent, was encountering similar difficulties, with comments like, "Good God Neil, you stung us for a fortune for his retirement gig and now you want to sting us for the reunion."

About three quarters of the way through recording the album came an awful combination of events: a) John had run out of money so they couldn't record anymore; b) Cheryl had left his employment; c) Neil delivered the list of bookings he could get for The Wimp And The Wild Tour.

"You don't get any better," said Willy, as he packed up his instruments in the studio. And yet again the duo split up.

There was one track on Side Wild of the unfinished album called 'The Last Of The Mohicans'. It was quite catchy, and captured the rough punky humour that had served the duo so well 10 years before. It also showed that even in adversity Otway was still capable of humour:

The last time I saw Judy
She was dancing with the Slug
The lead singer from a punk band called
Vomit Tastes So Good
She's the last of the Mohicans
The last of the Mohicans
The last of the reminders
Of the songs of yesterday

"Well at least we've got a hit out of this little venture," John told Chris. "That'll pay for the builders."

Chris did not agree, and neither did WEA when they heard it. "We are quite happy for John to approach other companies with this product," they said. "He can regard himself as being free from any contractual obligations."

The only record company that did think that 'Mohicans' was worth a shot was V.M. Records, a company based in a small village several miles outside Oxford. However, their budget was so limited that they could only issue it in a brown paper bag as opposed to a proper cover.

On the failure of yet another single, John announced to the occupants of the convertable flat that, "It is now essential that we commence building work as speedily as possible, in order to capitalise on the property developing and make some money."

Chris was told that he would have to lend John his share of the cost of the building expenses to convert their maisonnette. "It's OK," John said, "As soon as we've converted this place, I'll get another mortgage. We're making such a mint out of this developing that a few grand either way won't make much of a difference."

And so the builders moved into the maisonnette and proceeded to demolish it. John went back to gigging and the venues that were prepared to take Otway without Barrett were salvaged from The Wimp And The Wild Tour. During John's retirement, Robin his old guitarist had joined a band with a proper recording deal, and so John teamed up with a guitarist he knew from The Warrington pub, Ronnie Caryl. Ronnie had worked with many bands including Genesis and Joe Brown. Why he should want to work with Otway is a mystery.

"It's not much of a mystery," says Ronnie, "I was broke and Genesis didn't need a guitarist at the time. John asked me to join for a month which is turning into a year. A bit like a prison sentence but not as much fun."

Another person John asked to join for the 52-week month was Peter Bullick, a roadie he had used the couple of times

Patrice was too tired to keep up the heavy gigging schedule. "A roadie eh? What about manager, accountant, tour manager, relief guitarist and caterer?" says Peter.

"Peter came in pretty handy," says John. "Patrice had liked my retirement, as it meant she did not have to drive and pack gear continually and she refused to go back to it. I s'pose Peter took over where she left off."

By Christmas, disaster struck with a severity that completely validates the theory that just when you think things can't get any worse, they invariably do. It started a few days after the builders had more or less finished Chris and Karen's flat and turned the part of the maisonnette that was to be the Otways' home into a building site.

When they had bought the place, John had insisted that he and Patrice should have the top floor. "That way we can put a dormer-window in the roof and do a loft conversion and have one more room than Chris," he said.

And Keith and Paul, the builders, to his instructions, wasted no time in making huge holes in the roof and ceiling, and hoisted a huge staircase up into the top floor of the building.

The property that the foursome had purchased was at one time a council house, and a council tenant still resided on the ground floor. The tenant had complained to the council about the noise and inconvenience of the work being carried out above his home.

"What work?" asked the council, and sent an official around to investigate. "What on earth...?" he exploded as he walked up the stairs and saw what had once been a luxury maisonnette, and was now an almost completed one-bedroom flat with an adjacent building site.

"What on earth have you done?" he kept muttering as he rushed out of the building, only to return within five minutes with a legal document that, amongst other things said that the building work must stop with immediate effect. "I don't understand," said John, both bemused and close to tears. "Well speak to our lawyers," the official replied.

When Otway did speak to the lawyers it was like a nightmare. "You haven't read your lease, have you?" they said. Under the terms of the lease that our developers had purchased, it quite fundamentally stated that under no circumstances would the council allow the property to be developed. Furthermore, the loft and the roof space with the gaping holes did not even belong to them.

"I don't know what we're going to do about this," the council said, "but you certainly can't do any more building work until it's sorted out, and that could take years."

For Patrice it was the last straw. After six years of marriage to John in which she, more than anyone, had been closest to all of his various adventures, living in a flat where one could lie back and look at the stars was not as romantic as it sounds. She packed her few belongings and caught a plane back home to Canada and left him.

Otway was devastated. It is often said that things happen in threes, and in this case they did. They could just as easily happened in twos, but in this case John seemed hell-bent on heading for total disaster, and so as well as his home and his marriage, for reasons best known to himself he decided to throw his work in for good measure.

It started with a row over commissions with Neil Smith who, as Otway's agent, had done as much as possible to keep John earning a living with his live work.

"Well, he wanted to take the agency commission out of the gig money the week before Christmas," says Otway. "Otway owed the agency thousands, it was the week before Christmas and I needed the commission," says Neil.

A lot of the shows that John had been doing were on the London Pub Rock circuit. "Anyone can book those," John told Neil, and he and his agent agreed to end their business relationship. Peter Bullick, the roadie, ended up being his agent as well as everything else. That Christmas of 1987, 10 years on from John's best Christmas, he had his worst.

Neville Farmer had been a long standing friend of John's. He was a journalist that Otway had been introduced to by Roadie Lee years ago. He was also a drinker in The Warrington, John's favourite watering hole. "Yeah, he did look a mess round that time," Neville says. "He'd started drinking pretty heavily. He'd stopped caring for himself and you could tell something was wrong. Since he'd been acting, his hair had always been quite short, that Christmas it got long again and sort of stuck out around the ears. I realised then that he must have normally dyed it, because it looked decidedly grey.

"Anyhow, I couldn't go home for Christmas and I invited a bunch of other people, who were not going home for Yuletide, for a feast at my flat. I invited Otway too, 'cause he said that he couldn't face going home that year.

"He and Peter Bullick came round, and while we were watching *Terms Of Endearment* sneaked into the kitchen and polished off a whole bottle of 14-year old vintage port that I'd been saving to go with the Stilton."

"Well you can't blame me for not wanting to watch *Terms Of Endearment*, a film about marriage problems, at that time," explains John.

Karen Lawrence, a glassblower, and friend of Otway's since *Verbal Diary* days, recalls the mess he was in at that time. "He kind of turned up on my doorstep. He always looked as if he needed looking after, but I was actually worried about him. I offered to help him dye his hair back to brown and organise a trim for him."

"I did get a bit suicidal at that point, but I thought that things could be worse," says John. "I can't remember how I managed to think things could be worse, but I think it had something to do with the gigs I was getting Peter to book in. At least there were those."

John had told Peter how easy it was to book gigs. "You just phone the pubs up and say 'How about booking Otway?'" then sat him next to a phone. Surprisingly, within a couple of days Peter had managed to book 25 London Pubs, 18 of them in one month.

Neil Smith had been very selective in booking John's London shows. Neil understood that most people who saw him regularly could not stomach his show more frequently than a couple of times a month. As Otway was to discover, 18 was an overdose.

Neil had also ensured that John was always paid a guaranteed fee for his shows. Otway had told Peter not to bother with a guarantee and take a percentage of the door money. "Loads of people turn up to see me play," he said.

CHAPTER 34

Our story ends on April 16, 1988. Otway had played a pub in Camden town the previous night, he was on a percentage of the door, and three people had turned up to see him. John had been unable to pay either Ronnie his guitarist or Peter Bullick.

"John was totally depressed," says Peter. "He had somehow always looked optimistic. Even through the toughest times he would say, 'I know it's going to be alright, one way or another I'm going to be a star.' But that night he looked like a failure and I was worried about him.

"I nipped back to my flat, got the bottle of duty free Scotch I'd saved from my holidays, and stayed up all night drinking it with him round his flat." "Well it was actually Chris and Karen's flat," says John. "My flat was still a building site."

As opposed to Otway's disastrous time, for Chris France things couldn't have been better. Since the beginning of that year, Chris' record company, Music Of Life, had started having hit records. They had signed Derek B, who got a Top 20 hit, and Simon Harris, his partner, who had another with 'Bass How Low Can You Go'. "Things were going well for me," Chris says, "and I'd forgiven John for the property developing thing. I mean, I should have known better than to get involved with one of his schemes. Anyway, my flat was finished and I'd got the money to decorate it and furnish it properly. It didn't make too much of a difference to me that it was going to take some time before the building work got sorted out.

"I felt a bit sorry for John upstairs though. He was living on a sofa-bed in the one room that had no hole in the ceiling, even though part of the wall was missing. As my flat seemed to get more and more like a luxury apartment, his looked, and knowing Otway probably got, more and more like a demolition site.

"He didn't have any bathroom or kitchen up there, so I used to let him use mine, and as I was away most weekends he used the living room as well and watched the telly.

"It worked out all right. The only time we had words was when I wanted to stick up my new gold records in the bathroom and John said that he couldn't face looking at them first thing in the morning. I suppose I can see his point about that."

So there sat John and Peter in the newly furnished and decorated flat, discussing how on earth Otway could rescue himself now his marriage, home and career were all in ruins. No answer came that night. They continued drinking and such was the depths of despair that alcohol had no effect and they remained sober. All through the morning. Still no answer.

At lunchtime, they decided to go up The Warrington. "I get my best ideas in pubs anyway," John told Peter.

At last once again the rare event occurred, and Otway was right. Neville was in the pub. As a free-lance journalist he had been scouting around and talking to people who were likely to supply him with work.

"I was talking to a publisher last night, who's desperate for music-related books," he mentioned in passing. Otway's ears pricked up. "What if I wrote an Otway one?" John suggested.

"Heavens above Otway," Neville laughed. "If you wrote a book with all your disasters and cock-ups in, you'd sell a million." "Honest?" said John.

CHAPTER
35

It is 4th September 1988.

"Chris?" says John.

"Yes," says Mr. France warily.

"I've just finished this book that Neville Farmer reckons will sell millions, and I need some sort of financial help to publish it. I was thinking..."

ACKNOWLEDGEMENTS

I put the whole book in the third person. I found it impossible to write about myself in the first person, not because I'm modest – I just found it difficult to write lines like "Out of all possible options I chose the most ridiculous" and discovered that "Otway's course of action was, of course, predictable" said the same thing but did not make me feel quite as bad writing it.

My well thumbed copy of *How To Make A Fortune Out Of Writing* informs me that: "Publishers as a rule read a book before publishing it." I therefore feel particularly thankful to Omnibus for taking this book and to Dave Clarke for introducing me to them.

I'd like to thank John Breen who took the photograph on the front cover – would you believe that this picture was a publicity shot for my sponsors Shure Microphones! Thanks must also go to Andy Wood to H.W.International for its use.

My thanks go to Jim Driver, Maurice Bacon and Neville Farmer, and also to Karen Lawrence who put up with me becoming an author.

Sounds review reprinted courtesy of: Spotlight Publications.

Lyrics reprinted courtesy of: And Sons Music Ltd ('Trying Times', 'Dreaming Babies', 'Gypsy', 'Baby's In The Club', 'Can't Complain', 'Geneve', 'Cry, Cry', 'Day After Day' & 'Montreal'); And Son Music Ltd/ATV Music Ltd ('Headbutts'); and Bacon Empire Publishing Ltd ('Last Of The Mohicans').

UK LPS

JOHN OTWAY & WILD WILLY BARRETT

John Otway & Wild Willy Barrett
Extracked Records EXLP 1, 1977
Re-released on Polydor, 2383 453, 1977

Side 1: Misty Mountain/Murder Man/If I Did/
Racing Cars (Jet Spotter Of The Track)/
Louisa On A Horse/Gypsy
Side 2: Really Free/Bluey Green/
Cheryl's Going Home/Trying Times/Geneve

DEEP & MEANINGLESS

John Otway & Wild Willy Barrett
Polydor, 2383 501, 1978

Side 1: Place Farm Way/To Ann/Beware Of
The Flowers ('Cause I'm Sure They're Going
To Get You Yeh!)/The Alamo/Oh My Body Is
Making Me
Side 2: Josephine/Schnott/Riders In The Sky;
Running From The Law/Riders In The Sky/
I Wouldn't Wish It On You/Can't Complain

WHERE DID I GO RIGHT?

John Otway
Polydor, 2383 532, 1979

Side 1: Makes Good Music/It's A Pain/
Blue Eyes Of The Belle/Best Dream
Side 2: What A Woman/Frightened And
Scared/Waiting (Waiting For You)/
Hurting Her More/The Highwayman

WAY & BAR

John Otway & Wild Willy Barrett
Polydor, 2383 581, 1980

Side 1: Birthday Boy/D.K.50-80/
Cry Cry/21 Days/Medieval Dance
Side 2: Body Talk/Baby's In The Club/
Liberty Valence/When Love's In Bloom/
Day After Day/ Come Back Darling

GONE WITH THE BIN
(The Best of Otway & Barrett)

John Otway & Wild Willy Barrett
Polydor, POLS 1039, 1981

Side 1: Beware Of The Flowers ('Cause I'm
Sure They're Going To Get You Yeh!)/
Racing Cars (Jet Spotter Of The Track)/
Oh My Body Is Making Me/Riders In The Sky;
Running From The Law/Riders In The Sky/
Cheryl's Going Home/Birthday Boy/Geneve
Side 2: Really Free/D.K. 50-80/Louisa On A
Horse/Body Talk/Liberty Valence/Baby's In
The Club/I Did It Otway

ALL BALLS & NO WILLY

John Otway
Empire Records, HAMLP 1, 1982

Side 1: In Dreams/Too Much Air Not Enough
Oxygen/Telex/Montreal/Baby It's The Real
Thing/Turn Off Your Dreams (Don't Watch The
Nightmare)
Side 2: Mass Communication/House Is
Burning/Halloween/Nothing's Gone (Except
Number One)/Middle Of Winter

GREATEST HITS

John Otway & Wild Willy Barrett
Strike Back Records, SBR 4LP, 1986

Side 1: Really Free/InDreams/Turning Point/
Geneve/Mass Communication
Side 2: Beware Of The Flowers ('Cause I'm
Sure They're Going To Get You Yeh!)/Green
Green Grass Of Home/House Is Burning/
Montreal/You Ain't Seen Nothing Yet/
Middle Of Winter

THE WIMP & THE WILD

John Otway & Wild Willy Barrett
VM Records, VM 7, 1989

Side Wimp: The Wimp/Best Dream/Fashion/
Volunteer/Blockbuster/Separated
Side Wild: The Wild/House Of The Rising Sun/
Last Of The Mohicans/I Believe/I Am A Lion/
Focke Wulf

UK SINGLES

MISTY MOUNTAIN/GYPSY
John Otway
County Recording Service, COUN215, 1972

MURDER MAN/IF I DID
John Otway & Wild Willy Barrett
Track Records, 2094 111, 1973

LOUISA ON A HORSE/
BEWARE OF THE FLOWERS
John Otway
Viking Records, YRS CF 01, 1975

LOUISA ON A HORSE/MISTY MOUNTAIN
John Otway & Wild Willy Barrett
Track Records, 2094 133, 1976

RACING CARS (Jet Spotter Of The Track)/
RUNNING FROM THE LAW
John Otway & Wild Willy Barrett
Polydor, 2058 916, 1977

REALLY FREE/
BEWARE OF THE FLOWERS
John Otway & Wild Willy Barrett
Polydor, 2058 951, 1977

GENEVE/IT'S A LONG LONG TIME SINCE
I HEARD HOMESTEAD ON THE FARM
John Otway & Wild Willy Barrett
Polydor, 2059 001, 1978

BABY'S IN THE CLUB/
JULIE JULIE JULIE
John Otway
Polydor, 2059 060, 1978

FRIGHTENED & SCARED/
ARE YOU ON MY SIDE
John Otway
Polydor, 2059 105, 1979

D.K.50-80/HOMESTEAD ON THE FARM;
IT'S A LONG LONG TIME SINCE I HEARD
HOMESTEAD ON THE FARM
John Otway & Wild Willy Barrett
Polydor, 2059 250, 1980

GREEN GREEN GRASS OF HOME/
WEDNESDAY CLUB
John Otway
Stiff Records, BUY 101, 1980

TURNING POINT/
TOO MUCH AIR NOT ENOUGH OXYGEN
John Otway
Stiff Records, BUY 115, 1981

HEADBUTTS/
LIVE VERSION OF HEADBUTTS
John Otway & Wild Willy Barrett
Stiff Indie, BUY A LOT, 1981

IN DREAMS/
YOU AIN'T SEEN NOTHING YET
John Otway
Empire Records, HAM 3, 1982

MASS COMMUNICATION/
BABY IT'S THE REAL THING
John Otway
Empire Records, HAM 6, 1983

MIDDLE OF WINTER/
MAKES ME SEE RED
John Otway
Strike Back Records, SBR 1, 1983

THE NEW JERUSALEM/THE TYGER
John Otway
WEA Records, YZ 95, 1986

WHOOPS APOCALYPSE/LOSING
John Otway
WEA Records, YZ 111, 1987

THE LAST OF THE MOHICANS/
FASHION
John Otway & Wild Willy Barrett
VM Records, VMS 6, 1987

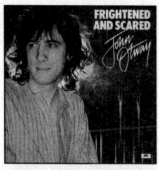

12 INCH EP

12 STITCH
John Otway & Wild Willy Barrett
Empire Records, HAM 5T, 1982
Side 1: Headbutts Live At Capitol Radio/
Best Dream 'Jingle'/Auld Lang Sammy
Side 2: Headbutts 'Jingle'/Headbutts
'Original Version'/Racing Cars 'Jingle'

USA & CANADA LPs

DEEP THOUGHT
John Otway
Stiff America, USE 5, 1980

Side 1: Liberty Valence/Body Talk/D.K. 50-80/
Cry Cry/Day After Day
Side 2: Beware Of The Flowers ('Cause I'm
Sure They're Going To Get You Yeh!)/
Murder Man/Really Free/Geneve/
Louisa On A Horse/Can't Complain/
Cheryl's Going Home

I DID IT OTWAY
John Otway & Wild Willy Barrett
Stiff Canada, RIP209, 1981

Side 1: Makes Good Music/Josephine/
If I Did/Running From The Law/I Did It Otway
Side 2: Headbutts/Turning Point/
Green Green Grass Of Home/Misty Mountain/
The Highwayman

USA & CANADA SINGLES & EPs

MURDER MAN/IF I DID
John Otway & Wild Willy Barrett
MCA Records, MCA 40081, 1973

**LIBERTY VALENCE/BIRTHDAY BOY/
RACING CARS (Jet Spotter Of The Track)**
John Otway
Stiff America, OWN 2EP, 1980, (USA)
Stiff Epic, E48415, 1980, (Canada)

I DID IT OTWAY (12 INCH EP)
John Otway & Wild Willy Barrett
Stiff America, NEW 3, 1981
Side 1: Running From The Law/
Turning Point/Headbutts
Side 2: Green Green Grass Of Home/
The Highwayman/I Did It Otway

TRACKS ON SAMPLERS

**BEWARE OF THE FLOWERS &
REALLY FREE**
John Otway & Wild Willy Barrett
20 Of Another Kind
Polydor, POLS 1006, 1979

THE MAN WHO SHOT LIBERTY VALENCE
John Otway
The Last Stiff Compilation
Stiff America, USE 3, 1980

MINE TONIGHT
John Otway
Miniatures LP
Pipe Records, PIPE 2, 1980

CHERYL'S GOING HOME
John Otway
Urgh A Music War
A&M Records, AMLX 64692, 1981

MISCELLANEOUS

OTWAY & BARRETT
LIVE AT THE ROUNDHOUSE
John Otway & Wild Willy Barrett
Limited edition of 250 numbered albums, 1977
White label catalogue no. OBL 1
Side 1: Slewfoot/Only A Hobo/Really Free/
Fire On The Mountain/Geneve/
Beware Of The Flowers ('Cause I'm Sure
They're Going To Get You Yeh!)
Side 2: Running From The Law/
Cheryl's Going Home/Down The Road/
Racing Cars (Jet Spotter Of The Track)

RACING CARS (Jet Spotter Of The Track)/
DOWN THE ROAD
John Otway & Wild Willy Barrett
Free single issued with the first 2000 copies
of DEEP AND MEANINGLESS LP
Polydor, OT 1, 1978

WHERE DID I GO RIGHT?
John Otway
Radio Promotional 12 inch EP
Polydor, OTTERS 1, 1979
Side 1: Frightened And Scared/Makes Good
Music
Side 2: It's A Pain/The Highwayman

THE NEW JERUSALEM/THE TYGER
John Otway
500 copies issued to press, radio and WEA to
encourage the label to release the single,
WEA, OTWEAY 1, 1986

BAGS OF FUN WITH BUSTER/
BAGS OF FUN WITH BUSTER
(Scrotal Scratch Mix)
Johnny Japes and His Jesticles
(featuring John Otway)
Mail order single sold through Viz Magazine
Fulchester Records, VIZ 2, 1987

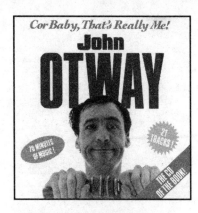

COR BABY THAT'S REALLY ME! CD

Over one hour's worth of flops mentioned in
this book released on CD. The tracks include:

Gypsy
John's ode to Mrs Clarke, his fortune teller,
released on County Recording Services,
John's own indie label.

Misty Mountain
John's first proper recording with
Pete Townshend at Olympic Studios
(previously unreleased version).

Murder Man
The first single on Track.

Really Free
The HIT.

Geneve
The version Willy called the "Walt Disney
Version" featuring Otway with a 100 piece
orchestra, unfortunately the follow-up single
to the HIT.

Beware Of The Flowers
The track that should have been the follow up
to the HIT but was used as its B-side.

Frightened And Scared
The Live In Your Living Room single.

D.K. 50/80
Back with Barrett for the tent tour on which
this epic was hyped to no.45 in the charts.

Headbutts
John's last near hit. Hear the yells of pain as
Willy smashes the Otway head against the
microphone.

Jerusalem
The record for which John signed WEA.

And many others...

TWO NEW BOOKS !

ROCK AND ROLL'S GREATEST FAILURE !

COMING IN 2010

I Did It OTWAY

Regrets, I've Had a Few!

THE NEXT EPISODE OF THE MICRO-STAR'S LIFE

deep&meaningless

the complete **john otway** lyrics

edited & compiled by **john haxby**

an enhanced reprint of the 1996 edition,
brought up-to-date with additional lyrics and photographs

for further details **www.johnotway.com**